AN UNTAMED TERRITORY

Darwin to Pine Creek 1913

Elsie Masson

ETT IMPRINT
Exile Bay

Published in Imprint Classics by ETT Imprint, Exile Bay 2026

First published as An Untamed Territory: The Northern Territory of Australia by Elsie R. Masson (Macmillan, London 1915)

ETT IMPRINT
PO Box R1906
Royal Exchange NSW 1225
Australia

First electronic edition ETT Imprint 2026

ISBN 978-1-923527-30-0 (paper)
ISBN 978-1-923527-31-7 (ebook)

Cover: The author when governess at the Gilruth household, Darwin 1913

Cover and design by Tom Thompson

Dedication

TO
MY FRIENDS
DR. J. A. GILRUTH AND MRS. GILRUTH
THIS BOOK
IS MOST AFFECTIONATELY DEDICATED

Mrs Gilruth, Dr Gilruth and Elsie Masson (right), Darwin 1913.

AUTHOR'S PREFACE

THE material for this book was collected in the Northern Territory during the years 1913 and 1914. I am deeply indebted to the Administrator of the Northern Territory and Mrs. Gilruth, who made it possible for me to study life in Darwin, and also to see something of the more outlying parts of the Territory, such as the country round the Darwin to Pine Creek Railway Line, the Daly River, the Alligator River, and the northern coast as far as the Roper River in the Gulf of Carpentaria.

My warmest thanks are due to Professor Baldwin Spencer of the University of Melbourne, both for the photographs he so kindly gave me and for his generous help and encouragement. I am indebted to the courtesy of the Hon. the Minister for External Affairs for the use of Figs. 1, 5, 13, and 14. I also wish to acknowledge with gratitude the great kindness of Dr. Mervyn Holmes of Darwin, to whom I owe most of the illustrations of this book, and to thank other friends for the use of some of their photographs.

Much of the contents of this book appeared first in the form of articles in the Melbourne *Argus*, the *Wellington Evening Post*, the Auckland *Herald*, the *Christchurch Press*, and the *Otago Daily Times*. It is by kind permission of the editors of these newspapers that I am able to republish.

MELBOURNE, 1914.

CONTENTS

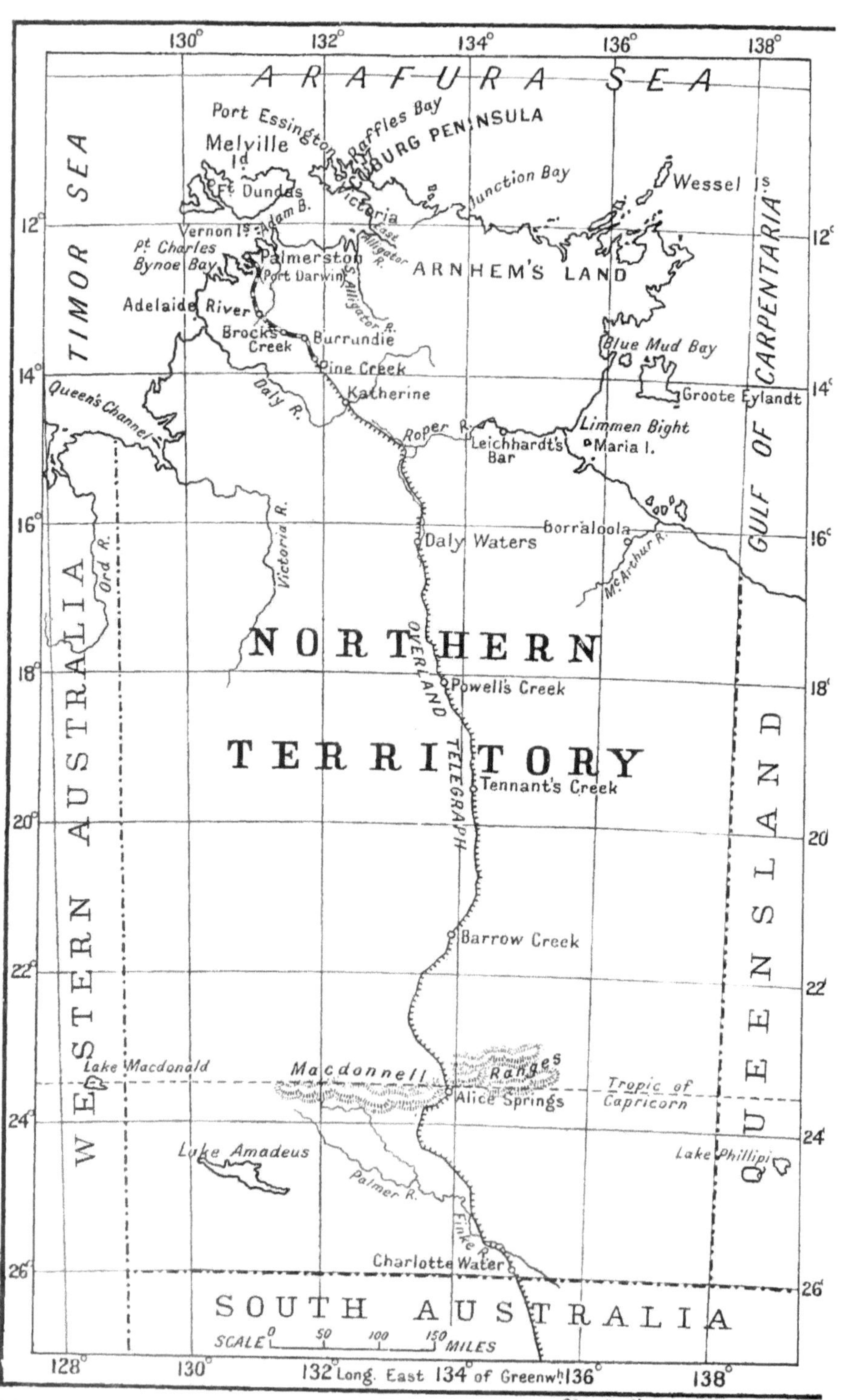

ARAFURA SEA
TIMOR SEA
Port Essington
Raffles Bay
COBURG PENINSULA
Melville Id
Ft Dundas
Junction Bay
Wessel Is
Vernon Is
Adam B.
Victoria
East Alligator R.
Pt Charles
Bynoe Bay
Palmerston
(Port Darwin)
S. Alligator R.
ARNHEM'S LAND
Adelaide River
Brocks Creek
Burrundie
Blue Mud Bay
Pine Creek
Katherine
Daly R.
Groote Eylandt
Queen's Channel
Roper R.
Leichhardt's Bar
Limmen Bight
Maria I.
GULF OF CARPENTARIA
Borraloola
Daly Waters
Ord R.
Victoria R.
McArthur R.
NORTHERN
TERRITORY
OVERLAND TELEGRAPH
Powell's Creek
Tennant's Creek
WESTERN AUSTRALIA
QUEENSLAND
Barrow Creek
Lake Macdonald
Macdonnell Ranges
Alice Springs
Tropic of Capricorn
Lake Amadeus
Lake Phillipi
Palmer R.
Finke R.
Charlotte Water
SOUTH AUSTRALIA
SCALE 0 50 100 150 MILES
128° 130° 132° Long. East 134° of Greenwh 136° 138°
12° 14° 16° 18° 20° 22° 24° 26°
Stanford's Geogl. Estabt. London

1 - Introductory

OF all parts of Australia, the least, although the longest, known is that huge expanse now called the Northern Territory. The Australian who visits it is surprised and strangely entranced with this portion of his continent. He is fascinated by the romance of the life and by the varied elements that compose it - the crude beginnings of white man's civilisation, the savage state of the Stone Age Aboriginal, and, foreign to both, the peculiar flavour of the East, reminding him that he is now within tropic regions. He finds an interest in these things quite apart from their political and national significance, but, to appreciate them to the full, he will do well to know first something of the extent of this vast land, of its past and of the nature of its country.

The coast line of the Northern Territory stretches for over a thousand miles, from the most southerly point of the Gulf of Carpentaria to the boundary of Western Australia, just beyond Queen's Channel, and inland it continues far beyond the tropic belt till it reaches Charlotte Waters, a station on the Overland Telegraph line, 1172 miles to the south. Its area of 523,620 square miles includes many varied kinds of scenery-moist tropical landscape watered by rivers flowing between banks of jungle; rich pastoral country; ridged land and sandy desert.

The rest of Australia has remained until lately indifferent to this part of the continent, if not blankly ignorant about it. It was so distant as to be almost forgotten; it was the hopeless unwanted land; to go there was to spend one's life in a stagnant backwater. It has held a curious position. It is part of Australia, and yet utterly remote from: the civilised states, separated from them by a fortnight's journey by sea; it is close to the East and yet not of the East. Only five days distant there is Java, with a swanning native population, with ancient temples and other relics of a historic past; to the north lies Manila, with palm trees and plantations; and in tell days' sail-less time than it takes to reach Sydney - there is Hong Kong, the very centre of the Orient. Yet in population, in scenery, and in animal life, it is not Eastern but Australian, and in its laws and customs it must conform with that Australia from which it is at present so remote.

It appears as if, of all parts of Australia, the Northern Territory will least readily submit to be civilised. All attempts made to subdue it seem to have been baffled, and the land to have relapsed into its indifference and mystery. Although its shores were touched upon and explored before the southern coasts were ever sighted, yet, when in the south the white man was established, and he and his herds were spreading inland, and the native dying out before them, the north remained unexploited, the home of the nomad savage.

For many years before the coming of white men the Malays had known and visited its shores. From Macassar, from the Celebes and other islands of the Arafura Sea, fleets of pro as, manned by dark keen-eyed, little pirates, swept down with the north-west wind. The boats were run up solitary beaches, or moored among mangroves in still creeks, while their crews camped nearby and collected trepang from the rocks. Their coming would be hailed by spirals of smoke rising in all directions, signals of the Aborigines to spread the news, and perhaps a mob of blacks would boldly make their camp in the neighbourhood, to be lured by gifts into serving the strangers, or more often to fall into deadly combat with them. When the south-easterly blew once more, the Malays loaded their proas with the dried trepang and sailed back to their islands. In spite of the difference of language and the probable contempt of the Malays for the Australian natives, it is hard to believe that they did not give the blacks some glimmerings of the world beyond, show them strange objects of civilised use and tell them tales of a white-skinned race. So that perhaps when instead of slight, brown-winged proas, high-pooped vessels crowded with 'white sail beat along the coast, and boat-loads of Hollanders pushed up the rivers in search of fresh water, their coming only fulfilled the prophecy of some distorted camp-fire legend.

The first to attempt to ascertain the truth about the Great South Land were the Dutch, Early Portuguese charts showed the outline of a country separated from Java by a narrow strait, and called Jave la Grande. There is, however, no written evidence to show that this represented Australia. The tradition of this great southern land-mass mass may have been founded upon the stories of the Malay islanders; or, mariners, blown far out of their course by the monsoonal storms, may have returned with tales of a strange coast. It is more than probable that the Portuguese navigators may have made genuine explorations along its shores, but that the story of their discoveries was jealously guarded for fear of Spanish rivalry. Whatever the truth, the Unknown Land of the south was hardly more than a legend till the advent of the Dutch.

The Dutch established themselves in the East Indies at the close of the sixteenth century, and in 1602 the Dutch East India Company was founded. Already it owned many rich possessions in the islands, and was desirous of seeing what further wealth lay over the seas. As early as 1606 the Dutch ship Duyphen had coasted down the eastern side of a great gulf (later named Carpentaria) but had "turned again" at Cape Keer Weer, before it reached the boundaries of what is now the Northern Territory. Zeachern, in the Mauritius, went farther, landed and named Arnhem's Land at the western point of the opening of the Gulf, and then left Australia probably little pleased at what he found. Jan Abel Tasman in command of three yachts - the Limmen, Zeemeuw, and De brak - voyaged up the western coast of the Gulf, passed Arnhem's Land and skirted along the northern shores. More than 150 years later, Flinders referred to the charts he left of his course and found them tally to a remarkable extent with his own observations.

This was the last voyage of importance made by the Dutch in Northern Territory waters. They left testimony of their exploration in the names that are still to be found all along the coast - Limmen Bight, Groote Eylandt, Arnhem's Land, Maria Island. But when once they had ascertained the nature of the country, they troubled themselves no more about it; and willingly let it slip into oblivion again. They had been thoroughly disappointed with their discoveries, and no wonder! They started out on their journeys with the highest hopes. Anything was possible. They might have found a wonderful people living in cities of white marble, clad in fine spun raiment with ornaments of silver and gold, growing spices and riding on elephants; instead they found lean-limbed black savages who threw spears and ran away. They might at the very least have come upon a land of gorgeous scenery, with noble ranges and mountain torrents, such as they had left in Java; instead there were plains of coarse grass, here and there low-topped hills, and rivers with banks of grey mud infested by alligators. They were soon decided that this country was no use to the Dutch East India Company, and of very little interest to the world in general, so the accounts of their discoveries remained buried amongst the company's papers, and North Australia passed out of the earth's history for more than another century.

The next attack upon the mysteries of this coast came from the south instead of from the north, and this time it was Englishmen and not Dutch who planted their flag on its shores and declared their sovereignty. In 1802 Matthew Flinders, in the *Investigator*, made a careful survey of both the east and west coasts of the Gulf, identifying his discoveries with those marked on the old Dutch charts, which till then had been regarded as more or less fanciful. Mangroves, mud-banked rivers, mosquitoes, crocodiles, skinny natives in dug-out canoes - all these he found just as the Dutch had before him. When he reached the Wessel Islands the state of his ship forced him to leave Australia and make for Timor. There remain the names he left, such as Blue Mud Bay, Dundas Island, and so on, while his charts, revised by more recent surveyors, are still used by navigators in the Gulf.

The first to be at all enthusiastic about the Territory was Captain Philip King, in command of the *Mermaid.* In 1821 he took up the survey of the coast where Flinders had left it and continued till he linked it up with his own exploration in the west. He was in particular greatly delighted with one fine harbour opening into the Coburg Peninsula, a harbour of deep water, firm cliffs and clean beaches. He was not the first to light upon it, for a fleet of Malay proas swept in before him and were evidently well acquainted with its waters. This harbour he named Essington, and looked forward confidently to a time when it would be an important commercial port.

The British Government now had a stirring of interest in its North Australian possessions, and it was thought well to establish settlements there, in order to begin colonisation, to encourage trade with the East, and to warn off any other nation, particularly the French. The history of these settlements is a melancholy one. The first attempt was semi-military, the detachment of marines which sailed from Sydney being accompanied by over a hundred colonists, four of whom were women. After a brief survey of Port Essington, their choice of a suitable site fell on Melville Island. From the first the settlement was mismanaged; trade there was none, the settlers were harried by natives, and for all the advance they were making in the colonisation of Northern Australia, they might equally well have remained in the temperate south. Fort Dundas, as they christened it, was partially abandoned, and a fresh attempt made at Raffles Bay on the mainland. Here things promised fairly well, but just at this point news reached the Home Government of the failure and distress at Melville Island, and immediately orders were dispatched, not only to complete the abandonment there, but also to leave the now successful Raffles Bay. There was a lull of ten years. Then the Government again became greatly perturbed at the idea of some other nationality laying claim to Northern Australia, on the ground that Britain was doing nothing to develop its resources. A settlement was established at Port Essington, this time purely military, though prospective settlers, who were to open the anticipated trade with the East, were offered the inducement of one-acre blocks in the "town of Victoria" at a seven years' lease for a nominal rent, or - still more tempting -"suburban" blocks of five acres. Perhaps if the Government had offered 50,000 acres for nothing a few bold spirits might have been induced to try and make some impression on the vast land. As it was, no one seemed willing to wrest a small suburban home out of the depths of untouched, tropical bush. Finally in 1848, worsted in the battle against conditions they did not understand, having done nothing to open up the country as they had hoped, the remains of the regiment at Port Essington were removed, and the forts and dwellings left to crumble away, in the triumphant bush.

Before this final abandonment, however, Stokes, in the *Beagle*, had been engaged in further explorations. He it was who discovered the two fine harbours to the west of the Vernon Islands, which he named respectively Port Bynoe, after the surgeon of his ship, and Port Darwin, after the brilliant, sea-sick young naturalist who accompanied him. Thus Darwin, the present capital of the Northern Territory, has the good fortune to bear the name of a great scientist of enduring fame, instead of, as might well have been, that of an ephemeral Lord of the Admiralty, or some rather uncomplimentary descriptive appellation.

Before the Port Essington settlement was finally abandoned, it welcomed Ludwig Leichardt, to whom its discomforts were luxuries after his journey of 3000 miles through unknown country. Eight months before he had started out from Queensland in charge of a small party of eight white men and two blackfellows, with cattle, horses, and stores. He struck north and skirted the shores of the Gulf of Carpentaria where one of his party, Gilbert, was speared by the natives. To this day the Aborigines of the Gulf country have a reputation for fierceness and treachery. On the western coast of the Gulf he discovered and named the fine Ropcr River, always associated with this first and successful expedition of Leichardt. Thence he went across country till he came upon the South and East Alligator Rivers, where he began to see signs amongst the natives that they had beheld, and had no fear of, white faces, associating them with tobacco and flour. "Ballanda, ballanda," they cried at his approach, a word which stands for "white man," and which Leichardt believes to have come straight to them from the Malays and to be no other than "Hollander." "Bal¬landa, ballanda," they still cry to the white visitors on the Alligator River. At last in December of 1845 he emerged on the settlement of Victoria, at Port Essington, and thence returned to the south, where great honour was done him. Three years later the natives of Coburg Peninsula had their country to themselves again; the last Ballanda had left; the Northern Territory had once more conquered in its struggle with the white man.

Fourteen years later, in 1862, South Australia rejoiced in the glorious news that one of her colonists, John McDouall Stuart, had crossed the continent from south to north. He had left the temperate zone, had traversed what seemed endless desert, had traversed what seemed endless desert, had watched its dreary features change to richer, tropic aspects, had revelled in the luxuriant green and plentiful life of northern river valleys, and had at length broken through the scrub on to a beach washed by the water of the ocean which was his goal. It, was a wonderful journey and opened up the possibility of an overland route, straight through the centre of Australia, which would link north with south. Stuart's reports of what he had seen gave promise of much prospective wealth, mineral and agricultural. South Australia, therefore, urged upon the Home Government that this immense tract should be attached to the colony. The suggestion was at first snubbed, as the Government seemed to think that something could still be done to civilise the north by the establishment of independent settlements. Then Queensland entered the field, representing that the north was far more allied to her in climate and in the nature of the country, and her claims seem to have found favour in the eyes of the British Government. South Australia was all indignation. Was the country, whose value had been made known by her. own citizen, in charge of an expedition dispatched and financed by her, which she therefore had made accessible by opening a way through the centre of the continent - was it to be withdrawn from her charge, and given to a state that up till then had never troubled about it? The Governor, the local Parlia¬ment, and the people said emphatically, No; and so impressed was the Home Government with their earnestness that it gave assent. In 1863 South Australia, with a population of 190,000, took over the responsi¬bility and development of the Northern Territory, confident that she had thereby greatly increased her wealth and resources - in fact, made her fortune.

Land sales took place almost immediately, and large tracts of land were sold both in South Australia and in London to companies which were promised that within five years it should be allotted and surveyed. Next, a Government Resident, accompanied by other officials and settlers, sailed to the north to select a capital. Against the advice of all those with him, the Resident chose Escape Cliffs in Adams Bay. It had been named by Stokes of the *Beagle* after a somewhat ridiculous episode had taken place there. Two of his men had been surprised on the beach by natives, who made war-like demonstrations and were all ready to throw their spears, when one of the men in desperation suddenly began to dance. The other followed his example, and the natives were so astonished and put out by this unexpected, behaviour that they lowered their spears and stood gazing till a boat-load of shipmates arrived to the rescue.

The other association that clings to Escape Cliffs is that of an unhappy settlement, Government Resident at war with his subordinates, natives and Europeans on unfriendly terms, and general discontent. The South Australian Government, which imagined everything was going merrily, was suddenly horrified at the arrival of *The Forlorn Hope,* a small boat in which some of the settlers, desperate at the mismanagement that they saw going on, had sailed all the thousands of miles from Escape Cliffs in order to take the news to South Australia. The Government was soon convinced of the failure of the new capital, the unsuitability of the site, and the indiscretions of its Resident. The Resident was at once recalled, new exploring parties were sent out, and finally Port Darwin was chosen as the most suitable position for the capital. The newly-made town was christened Palmerston, though it was more often called by the name of the harbour Port Darwin. In later years Palmerston was dropped, and the town is now always known as Darwin. Thus, after much delay, the first step had been taken; but in the meantime the land was no nearer being surveyed and apportioned, the five years' grace was exhausted, and shareholders were growing impatient. Some of the purchase money had to be refunded, and even the most enthusiastic felt the newly acquired Territory was not proving the tractable child that the parent colony had counted on.

The next few years, however, brought a brighter outlook. The new capital and the new Government Resident both proved a success. Goyder's survey party did valuable work, and at length the ballots for land could take place. Finally the great scheme of an Overland Telegraph from Adelaide to Port Darwin was set on foot.

A stranger arriving in Adelaide on the 22nd of August 1872, might have thought news had reached the town of some great military victory. The city was bright with flags and loud with bells; in the streets people shook hands vigorously and congratulated each other. It was indeed a victory they were thus celebrating - the victory of the Overland Telegraph, which had that day transmitted the first message from Port Darwin to Adelaide. The forces on one side conisted of a small party of white men, generalled by Charles Todd; on the other, of 1900 miles of unsurveyed country, the difficulty of obtaining supplies, frequent scarcity of water, and danger from savage tribes and sickness. Adelaide rejoiced over the success of its scheme; Port Darwin rejoiced because it was now in close, daily touch with the south, and could no longer remain in utter ignorance for many weeks at a time of what the civilised world was doing and thinking. When shortly afterwards the cable station was established there, the little outpost became an important connecting link between Australia and the Old World. Never again, whatever might happen to the Territory, could Port Darwin drop right out of mind nor be forgotten.

Other cable lines to other parts of Australia have detracted a little from this importance, but the value of the Overland Telegraph has never diminished. It is today the one definite line of civilisation that runs through the whole country. A man from out back will tell you that he lives "three weeks from the O.T."; the sight of its iron poles and thin streak of wire has often meant salvation to an overland traveller; up or down he knows that by following it he is sure to light upon a spot of habitation, the next telegraph station with its two officials, its small iron structure, and its flock of goats.

After the completion of the Overland Telegraph there came good times to the Territory, for minerals - gold, tin, and copper - were discovered, and there was a rush to the fields from other parts of Australia. Companies were formed and flourished for a time, but eventually came to nothing. Although the minerals were there in plenty, yet the natural disabilities of difficulty of transport and labour were increased by mismanagement and ignorance of conditions. The mining, which had given such promise, gradually petered out; the mines were deserted or left to a few fossicking Chinese, and the Northern Territory still kept its riches to itself.

South Australia tried every means in its power to ease the conditions in the north. Port Darwin was declared a free port, and legislation was passed to encourage sugar-growing. Unfortunately the De Lissa Ale Company, which started a sugar plantation, had no success with its venture and ultimately failed altogether.

The question of labour in the north was at first answered by the importation of Chinese. In 1874 the first were introduced, and soon every ship from the East brought numbers of coolies from Southern China, to whom the Northern Territory gave wealth compared to the poverty that they had left behind. At first welcome, after a while this influx of Asiatics became alarming, and, only fourteen years after the first agitation for their introduction, it was found wise to take measures to restrict it by imposing a poll-tax upon each one imported. Nowadays, of course, owing to the White Australia policy, no more are admitted, and the number of Chinese in the Territory has now shrunk till it no longer exceeds the European population. But in the 'eighties there were thousands of them. They worked as miners, as servants, as labourers, and lastly were employed in large numbers in the construction of the first portion of the Overland Railway from Palmerston to Pine Creek.

The scheme of the Overland Railway was a great and worthy one. It was to cross the continent from north to south, and open a way for people and goods into the heart of the Territory. Civilisation was to follow its track, and the final subjection of the Northern Territory was to be completed. It was begun in 1886, and, in 1887, the Overland Telegraph carried the news to Adelaide that the wife of the Government Resident at Palmerston "in a neat speech and breaking a bottle of champagne" had christened the first engine "The Port Darwin," after which the white population had been taken for its first ride along the line. This glorious beginning promised well, but alas! when the railway reached Pine Creek, a mining township and telegraph station 147 miles inland, it stopped, and all further construction was abandoned. Twice a week ever since, a train has run from Port Darwin to Pine Creek; once a fortnight ever since, a train has run from

Adelaide to Oodnadatta. There they have faced each other over the thousand intervening miles, and then turned tail and gone back again.

The making of the railway was the last decisive action on the part of South Australia; its abandonment was a sign that she had thrown up the sponge, realising that not only time and continuous effort but also the expenditure of more money than she could afford, would be necessary to subdue the obdurate north.

Once again the Northern Territory had won, though it emerged from battle badly wounded, by the Overland Telegraph, by the firm establishment of Palmerston, and by the little railway. Now a new enemy gathered its forces together and opened a fresh campaign. In 1907 the Federal Government of the Commonwealth of Australia took over the responsibility of the Northern Territory, with its population of 1500 Europeans, the same number of coloured people, and, roughly speaking, 40,000 Aborigines. Henceforward it became Federal ground, attached to no State, sending no representatives to any Parliament, and, like the rest of the Commonwealth, closed to all Asiatics. In 1912 an Administrator, Dr. J. A. Gilruth, and other officials, arrived in the Territory to tackle and solve the great problem which includes so many small ones - how may this vast land be civilised and settled, how may its wealth be exploited, keeping it at the same time a white man's country? The Northern Territory will fight hard, and some prophesy that it will triumph again; but for the most part those who watch the struggle feel that the old warrior has met its match and must yield at last, though the victory will be no cheap one.

When the schemes of the Federal Government were set on foot and the work was begun, the Northern Territory suddenly leaped into public notice, and its future became the subject of much discussion in the south.

Yet this, the official and political side, is not the only one of interest; from the picturesque point of view the Territory is endlessly fascinating. Those that go there undergo a strange experience - not only do they travel many hundreds of miles by sea, but also they journey sixty years into the past, into the old Australia of the early days before the gold rush, an Australia which has long passed away in the south but which still lingers in the wild, intractable Northern Territory.

The author, Darwin 1913.

2 - A WOMAN'S LIFE IN DARWIN

ON the woman, no less than on the man, depends the success of a great venture such as the civilisation and development of the Northern Territory. The prospect of better work, or the fascination of life in a more primitive community, has drawn him there. The wife, on the other hand, goes because he goes, and not because the life appeals especially to her nature. Therefore there is still more necessity for her to make up her mind that she will endure discomfort without grumbling and set herself to solve the small problems of the home, which are all part of the larger problems of the Territory.

The woman who leaves the south for Darwin has a very confused idea of what lies before her. She has heard many and varied accounts of the Northern Territory, most of them founded on little real knowledge and nearly all discouraging. "Surely you are not going to take the children to that awful hole?" most of her women friends exclaim, with a look which expresses plainly what a heartless mother they think her. Then follows a description of her future home as a burning land, full of fevers and insect pests, where food is bad and health lost after a few years' stay. Darwin itself is represented as a shadeless sun-blistered township, baking all day on a bare rock. While she is summoning up her courage to meet these conditions, another says to her: "Darwin? Oh, but it is a Paradise," and she is left in bewilderment. If she is wise, she forms no mental picture of the place, but waits till she is able to judge it for herself.

If she is well-advised, she will not start her journey to the Northern Territory till April, when the hot, wet months are past and the dry rainless season which lasts until October is begun. At this time, also, there is a fair certainty of a calm voyage, and a calm voyage is well worth while on the east coast of Australia. Shortly after leav¬ing Brisbane, the steamer passes inside the Great Barrier Reef, and sails past mile after mile of ridged coast line, softly wooded with lonely forest, and backed by mysterious mountain ranges. On all sides little purple islands rise out of the peacock-blue sea, revealing, as the boat passes by, hidden beaches, dark caves and rocky reefs crested with palms. There is a pause in the beautiful harbour of Cairns, then the shelter of the reef is left behind and a long swell from the south-east sets the steamer rolling. The next port is Thursday Island, a township of white houses spread over the side of a bare, rocky island. The place exists on its pearling, its trade in trepang or *beche-de-mer*, and its regiment of soldiers who stand between Australia and the millions of the East. Here the traveller from the south sees for the first time a really mixed population. The main street of the town is lined with neat Japanese and Chinese stores; at the corners stand groups of burly Aboriginals; Malay and Japanese pearlers hang over the verandahs of tiny, ramshackle houses; a native of New Guinea, with stiff, frizzy hair standing a foot high, strides down the road, and there are besides innumerable others of every shade of brown belonging to all or none of the races inhabiting the island.

Between Thursday Island and Darwin is the longest stretch of sea without a port. The water is colourless and oily, and it is in a haze of sticky heat that the newcomer gazes on her future home, the Northern 'Territory - a slip of blue land away on the horizon.

Early in the morning the steamer begins to go half speed, and, by the time the passengers are on deck, it is crawling slowly up the harbour of Darwin. The heat has disappeared, and a fresh, cool breeze is blowing over the sea. On all sides are low, green shores covered with mangroves which grow right into the water. A squat little sailing-boat with square, ribbed sails like withered leaves lies dead in the steamer's path. It is a Chinese sampan on the look-out for opium, which, in spite of ship's officers and customs, has been smuggled all the way down south and back again. A signal will be hoisted by the Chinese crew, something dropped over the stern, and presently the sampan will move slowly across the steamer's wake and then scud innocently away over the blue harbour water. Gradually the shores of the harbour rise to cliffs, the boat swings round the corner and there, in a bay between two headlands, lies Darwin.

Darwin first shows itself to the newcomer as anything but a treeless rock. It is a scattered collection of white roofs, pushing their way through masses of green foliage which covers the low cliffs and grows almost to the water's edge. Close to the shore arc half-submerged mangrove trees and all sorts of queer craft - sampans, long, black dug-out canoes, and dainty pearling luggers. In a short while the new arrival is driving along the wide, red road and Darwin is no longer a mystery to her. It is a small township, with a few buildings of solid stone and more of wood or galvanised iron, but saved from unsightliness by the verandahs enclosed with plaited bamboo and with bright shrubs showing through the open shutters. There is besides the street of dilapidated houses known as Chinatown. Since the Manchu dynasty fell, the pigtail has vanished from Darwin and embroidered robes arc no longer seen on feast days, but the blue coat and wide black trousers of the Chinese coolie are still adhered to. By late afternoon all the population of Chinatown is in the street. Wrinkled old men, whose hollow chests betray the opium smoker, peer slowly like ancient tortoises round the dark doorways of hovels, or drag themselves painfully across the street. Younger and burlier men lean against verandah posts, smoking long bamboo pipes. Children in blue jackets and pink trousers, their heads shaven except for one lick of hair in front, sit on the curb gazing solemnly in front of them as if they knew all the wisdom of the ages. Merriest of all are the little Chinese women, who stand with babies like tiny yellow Buddhas in their arms, smiling happily.

For the most part, the buildings are tailoring establishments, where hollow-chested China boys sit all day whirring at their machines, or else they are laundries where, through dark doorways, the owner can be seen swiftly ironing, or again they are stores. The stores are all alike-dark and smelling mustily of incense and dust. Two seats of polished bamboo guard the door, on which old Chinese lie and smoke, their knees drawn up to their chins. The shelves on the wall are covered with a curious collection of things - tins of biscuits, fans, tubes of tooth paste, bottles of aspirin and prints of Sun Yat Sen, all mixed together. In the dark background are rows of fruit jars, big baskets, and solid cedar tables, while over all this presides the crudely painted image of the joss.

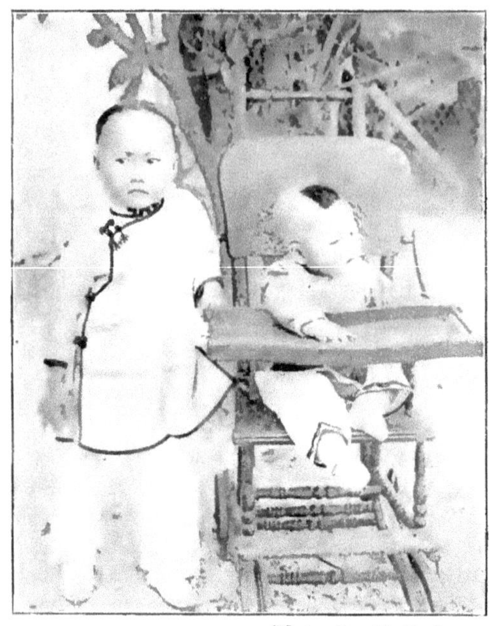

Photo, Dr. Maplestone.

CHILDREN OF CHINATOWN.

Photo, Dr. Mervyn Holmes.

CHIN QUE AVENUE, CHINATOWN, DARWIN.

On the outskirts of Chinatown is a blight of small hovels jumbled together where live the rest of the coloured population of Darwin. Even in her first rapid drive the newcomer sees people of every colour, until she feels as if she were turning the leaves of a book of patterns ranging from deepest chocolate to pale cream. Black Aboriginals throw spears on open grassed spaces between the houses; dusky Malays, short and sturdy, sit smoking by the roadway; children of all shades of brown peer with bright curious eyes round the tin walls of their homes; yellow, wrinkled Chinese, in blue silk trousers, carrying baskets slung on poles, pass at a shuffling trot. Before long she is in her own dwelling and her life as a woman of Darwin has begun.

The house where she finds herself is built of wood and the roof is of corrugated iron.

It is surrounded by a wide verandah enclosed by plaited bamboo and is decked with gay palms in pots. There are chairs, tables, books, and beds on the verandah, and before long she realises that this is an important part of the house. The rooms, which are covered with matting and contain only purely necessary furniture, are merely places in which to dress and keep one's clothes. The family lives, eats, and sleeps on the verandah, moving camp when the sun gets too hot on one side and opening the shutters to let in the breeze.

The house has not been inhabited of late and at first the new mistress has to wage an insect war. Food cannot be left half an hour on the table before ants swarm upon it; cockroaches, sometimes two or three inches long, make startling rushes from behind wardrobes; silver fish slither away swiftly when drawers are opened; mosquitoes make life a constant burden. Each pest has to be combated in a different way. The legs of every table and safe must be put in tins half full of water so that the ants cannot get to the food; daily sweepings and dustings hunt the cockroach from his lair, and after a wild stampede of the family in pursuit, armed with towels and pillows, he is generally caught; the silver fish are baulked by tying in bags of unbleached calico those clothes that are not in constant use. Worst pest of all, the mosquitoes, are also vanquished. Kerosene is poured into the tanks so that the larvae in the water suffocate, and old tins in the backyard half-filled with rain-water, where the mosquitoes breed thickly, are all buried. For a while the mosquitoes vanish; then they return more numerous than before. Every corner is searched for lying water with no success. Suddenly it is discovered that the water in the tins, which are the defence against the ants, has not been changed for a day or two, and is full of wriggling larvae. So it goes on, requiring constant vigilance, and for a time it seems as if these worries were to be permanent, but gradually, with cleanliness and order, the cockroaches, ants, silver fish, and mosquitoes leave for less molested quarters. So that first problem has now been faced and solved.

A surprise, and an agreeable one to the new arrival in Darwin, is the food. Of all the reports she has heard "down below" the only one which she really believed was that the inhabitants of Darwin lived on tinned meat and vegetables. And yet she finds that every day the freshest of beef can be bought at the butcher's, just as it is in the south. It is true that till lately mutton was the Christmas treat, and still the only word in the black's vocabulary for meat is "beef." At that time also ice was unheard of, and it was necessary to wait till the steamer came in to get a really cool drink. Now there are freezing works and the diet of beef can be varied, while fresh butter and ice can also be obtained.

For fruit and vegetables she relies on the fat old Chinaman, Ah Wung, who waddles daily to her door with a cheery "Mornin', Missis," and deposits his basket at her feet. The fruit is a disappointment, not in its quality but in its price. Pineapples, bananas, paw-paw - all are delicious; but the first two are almost as expensive as they are in Sydney or Melbourne, while the last is absurdly dear, considering how easily it grows round Darwin. It is no use trying to argue with Ah Wung. He remains affable but firm, knowing quite well that he has a monopoly of all the fruit grown around Darwin, and that it pays him to store it up to sell to the incoming steamer. The vegetables Ah Wung offers are travesties of English ones - beans nearly a yard in length, Chinese turnips and cabbage, and a strange white globe called egg fruit. "What for you no more grow English cabbage? " she asks in disgust. "Chinee cabbage more better, I think," answers Ah Wung imperturbably. The first time they are tried at table the family declares they taste like the smell in the interior of the Chinese joss-house, and emphatically refuse to touch them all.

Then one day someone shows her the special ways of preparing and cooking them, which make them quite as palatable as English vegetables, while the egg fruit is a delicious new dish. Ah Wung smiles a smile of bland triumph when the "Missis" begins to buy the despised Chinese vegetables again.

The wise housekeeper in Darwin rises early, gets work over while the morning is still fresh, rests during the hot part of the day, and, after four o'clock, goes out to take air and exercise. There are walks to be had on golden beaches fringed with cocoanut palms, or drives along red roads between a thick tangle of jungle to a white point of rock sticking out into the sea, stiffly set about with groups of pandanus. The sun sinks and life begins to stir. Wallabies dash away through the long grass, flying foxes flap through the branches of the trees, a wood-cart, drawn by a solemn black buffalo with a tan-coloured old Chinaman crawling alongside, passes on its way home; families of blacks wave cheerily as they march back to camp. Night follows sunset within a few minutes-cool, scented tropic night with the glimmer of stars on the water, and mingled sounds of the drone of a black's corroboree and shouts from pearling luggers.

There is only one newspaper in Darwin.

This publishes daily a small slip called an Extraordinary, which purports to give all the news of the day. Every week the paper comes out in full, and contains all the Extraordinaries of the past week reprinted, For the rest, it confines itself to comments on local events or to repeating what has been said of the Northern Territory in the south, and its comments on World's news are spasmodic. Mails arrive at irregular intervals, sometimes two or three boats calling from the south within a few days of each other, followed by a pause of three weeks without even one, During the pause the harbour is deserted and lifeless. Then it is telephoned from the jail, where a black prisoner has been on the watch, that the steamer is sighted. There is an hour's wait, and then suddenly the full, deep roar of the mail steamer breaks upon the silence and she slowly sails into sight, looking a monster to eyes that have grown accustomed to the small craft of Darwin. From the moment she drops anchor, the town is a distracted whirl. The whole population, white and yellow, swarms on to the pier, the white to amuse themselves with the sight of unknown faces, the yellow to visit their friends and cousins in the crew. All day from the wharf are to be heard the shunting of trucks, rattling of donkey engines, shouting of men and clanging of ship's bells. Business and officialdom is completely paralysed, and for everyone there are mails to be written and dispatched, and perhaps boat's passengers to be entertained. There is a period of restless suspense, while the mail is being sorted. If it is night, the little twinkling lights of hurricane lanterns can be seen hastening in from all directions towards the post office. The newsagent's cart passes, piled with papers - a hopeful sight - and is greeted with a cry of "Is the mail ready?" "Close up," comes the cheering answer. At last a bell is rung from the post office steps to announce that the mail is sorted, and presently the crowd of Whites, Chinese, Malays, and Japanese that has collected hastens away, bearing huge bundles of papers and letters. For an hour or so afterwards, everyone is revelling in the news of the distant world, revived by old interests, warmed by old battle cries. Then the savage cadence of a corroboree brings back the sharp realisation that one is in Darwin - cut off by thousands of miles from the rest of civilisation.

The newcomer's first experience of the climate of Darwin is in the dry season, when the days are so cool that she can hardly believe that the weather is not playing some trick upon her. Every day is bright and cloudless, with a fresh wind blowing over the blue harbour. At night a brilliant tropic moonlight glitters on the sea and the air is rich with warm scents. The roads about the town are thick with red dust, the grass in the bush is long and yellow, in bed at night a blanket is always welcome.

With the beginning of September comes a change. The days and nights grow steadily hotter. Yellow clouds lower on the horizon, the sea is a sullen greenish tint, the air heavy with the sense of something coming. Gusts of wind sweep up, whirling leaves and dust before them; thunder grumbles in the distance.

DARWIN.

A collection of white roofs pushing their way through masses of green foliage

A TYPICAL DARWIN STREET

Everything seems to be working up to a climax and still that climax will not come. Then, at last, a storm of rain rushes across the harbour and falls on the house, trampling the iron roof like a regiment of cavalry. The dreaded "wet" has now set in that is to send her home a white-faced wreck. But the newcomer has long ago found out that old Territorians prefer the wet season, and she soon begins to understand why. The red dust of the road settles and the country emerges from its dried chrysalis a brilliant green. The beauty of the place, the wonderful colour effects at sunset, the luxuriance of the foliage, all cast their spell upon her. Life begins to swarm again. Herds of wallaby and kangaroo feed at evening close in to the town, frogs croak an interminable chant, flying ants pile up in heaps round the lamps, gorgeous butterflies and dragon-flies flash their wings in the sun. The days are very hot and close till after rain, when a cool refreshing breeze blows over the damp earth. Often the rain is heralded by a terrific thunderstorm, when the whole world seems to crack about her ears and lightning flaps in her eyes like a blanket.

So the months slip by, the rain suddenly stops, the dry season begins again, and, with a start, she realises that a whole year has passed since, full of misgivings and apprehensions, she first gazed on the white roofs of Darwin from the steamer deck. During that year she has experienced some discomforts and many small worries; she has had moments of home-sickness and loneliness when she longed to take the first boat south; but in the end she has not been daunted. She realises with a thrill of pride that she may now call herself a woman of the Northern Territory.

3 - THE SERVANT QUESTION

OF all the problems of the Northern Territory that one which affects most deeply the women who go there is the problem of domestic service. Certainly this is not confined to the Territory, yet its difficulties are very different from those that present themselves in the southern states. There it is a question of finding and keeping white servants; in Darwin there are no white servants at all, Moreover, the supply of China boys is rapidly shrinking, and in consequence the wages are rising till a good Chinese cook will ask at least £8 a month. If the new arrival in the Territory can afford this, she is happy indeed, for her kitchen department will be competently and conscientiously looked after.

Cook is stout, beetle-brewed, and deep-¬voiced, always jovial and imperturbable in any circumstances, and an excellent chef. Through the kitchen window his black head can be seen bending over his saucepans, or his burly form, in white singlet, wide black trousers, and blue cummerbund, moving from oven to dresser with incredible swiftness. At the same time he pours out a flood of Chinese. Then his voice, which in speaking English is only a deep guttural, rolls up and down in a sonorous torrent of words, pausing every now and then for a deep-toned note on a long vowel till it sounds like the tuning up of the violins and cellos in an orchestra. His conversation is generally addressed to Chin Sing, the laundryman, who brings the washing to and fro from his little house in Chinatown. Chin Sing is lean, brown, and withered, like an old peanut. He looks as if he might at any moment slip through a crack in the verandah, and he frequently seats himself comfortably on a jam tin to have a talk with cook. Jokes fly between them, cook rolls with deep chuckles from one side of the kitchen to the other; Chin Sing cackles thinly, then seizes his bundle of washing and scuttles off as rapidly as a cockroach.

But it is becoming less and less likely that the new arrival in the Territory will be able to secure such a prize as a Chinese cook. More probably she will have to rely on herself and aboriginal help. It is very likely that her first choice of a black boy is a failure. George is not a native of Darwin, but he and some of his countrymen have paddled in a canoe all the way from their home on the Daly River to see a little town life in Darwin. He is a slender youth of about sixteen, with straight, black hair, a very narrow head, gloomy eyes, and an air of easy nonchalance very exasperating to the Missis. He is dressed in dirty khaki trousers, a blue shirt, and a bead collar of his own making.

The Mistress's troubles begin when she steps on to the verandah in the morning and looks round for George, who should long ago have begun his sweeping. Every evening she says to him, "Now, George, sun there," pointing sternly to the eastern horizon, "you get up, savvy?" Every evening George answers cheerfully, " Orright, Missis,' and every morning finds him fast asleep with a thick blue blanket pulled well up over his head. After being rudely disturbed, he strolls round to the verandah and begins dreamily sweeping. The Missis stands by directing the work. George cannot see why, because she makes him move one mat or one table and sweep under it, that should mean that all the other mats and tables must also be moved. Each one requires a fresh direction, so that George's sweeping needs a good deal of supervision.

George has no specified day off, but he takes one whenever he feels inclined, sometimes to the great inconvenience of the household. On his return, Boss "plenty growl." "What for you go out to-day?" he asks. "Corroboree - my brudders and sisters," answers George. He seems to have an endless, supply of brothers and sisters, who pass their days in holding corroborees. "Want go see my sister to-day, Missis," he says. "Where your sister?" "He longa hospital." "What name your sister?" asks a suspicious Missis. A long pause. " Maudie, I think," answers George carelessly. The Missis at last tells George he really must not go to any more corroborees, whereupon George retaliates by bringing the corroborees there. Suddenly there is a burst of noise from the backyard, clapping of hands, buzzing of bamboo pipes, and endless chanting of a monotonous refrain varied by shrieks of laughter. After an hour of this the Boss brings the corroboree to an end. George, however, invites his friends to spend the night, and next morning in the backyard there are five sleeping blacks under blue blankets instead of one.

George suddenly seems to be becoming more brisk and diligent in his work. For a few days he is so good that the Missis decides he is really worth keeping, and, if worth keeping, deserving of more respectable clothing. So she buys him a pair of dungarees, a leather belt, two khaki shirts, and a red handkerchief. "I give you these because you good boy," she explains graciously. "Orright, Missis," he answers tersely. Next morning he presents himself in all his new grandeur and says, without any preliminaries, "Missis, me go out bush to-morra." "What, George?" exclaims a startled Missis. "Go back longa my country to-morra," he repeats. "How you go?" asks the Missis weakly. "Canoe." There is nothing more to be said. George has bush fever, and if the whole police force of Darwin were called out it could not keep him back. The Missis stands absolutely taken aback, not knowing what to say next. Memories of occasions not unlike this in the south cross her mind, and she half expects him to add that his mother has broken her leg and would she please give him a reference, when George puts an end to the matter by saying, with an encouraging smile, "Four moon my come back longa Darwin, sit down longa you, Missis." So George goes back to the life of a primitive savage, to weird corroborees by moonlight in the silent bush, to long hunts after tucker, to the learning of strange tribal magic from white-haired warriors back to the Stone Age for four moons.

After this the Missis wisely decides to employ only Larakia blacks whose country is Darwin. She engages one, and gets a family. There is Paddy, short and sturdy, with a friendly grin under the bristling moustache, who addresses the Boss and Missis equally as Sir"; there is his lubra, Nellie, and his baby, Rita, who come to "sit down lazy" while Paddy works. Soon Nellie expresses a wish to work also, and before long becomes of infinite value. Although she too has to be told the same thing day after day, and, if given more than one direction at a time, sits down cheerfully to do nothing, yet she works with a will, and soon learns to sweep, to dust, to scrub, to wash up and to do laundry work. Chin Sing's price is "slippence piecee," that is to say, threepence is paid for each article, whether it be a sheet or a handkerchief. Therefore it is well worth while teaching Nellie to wash small things, even if, one day when the mistress's back is turned, she burns holes in half a dozen handkerchiefs, or becomes so fascinated with wielding the blue bag that the clothes all return from the wash bright cobalt in colour.

At first the Missis thinks Nellie the most hideous object she has ever seen, with her flat nose, huge lips, from which always hangs a big black pipe, and her straggling locks. Soon she forgets her first repulsion, and finds the good-humoured face almost comely, and an easy grace beneath the ugly one-piece cotton dress. This grace vanishes completely when Nellie appears in her "best," which consists in a man's straw hat, pulled down to her eyebrows, a faded cloth jacket, which looks as if it must have belonged to a smart coat and skirt of the early 'eighties, and a soiled white petticoat. The Missis promptly presents her with a pretty, blue cotton dress, and adds a brush and comb, so that Nellie appears looking neat and picturesque, with her hair smoothed down and bound round with red wool fastened in a large bob in the middle of her forehead.

Rita is a fat healthy child, who crawls about unclad on the flats of her hands and feet, constantly making the Missis think that there is a small brown bear in the yard. She sits up and claps her hands together, as she has already learned to do at corroborees. " Rita. killem finger," says Nellie proudly.

She shares her parents' tucker-very sweet tea, meat and bread-which they eat on the back verandah, chattering merrily to each other about Heaven knows what.

They do not live at the house, but at the camp of natives at Kahlin Beach a mile away. Every evening at sundown the little family passes out of the garden. First Paddy strides ahead with the billy in one hand and a bundle of spears in the other; then Nellie, carrying the rest of the burdens, with Rita perched on her shoulders, gazing gravely on the world. They cry the Larakia good-bye as they go, -" Maa-maak, Missis, maa-ammk, Boss," and swing briskly through the gate.

Simple, merry folk, docile but never cringing, frequently exasperating but endlessly amusing, they know a sure way to gain affection, the way of a responsive, artless child. Let it be acknowledged that, in smoothing the domestic path of the women, they too are taking part in the development of their own country.

Photo. Dr. Mervyn Holmes.

A DARWIN HOUSE BOY.

COCOANUT PALMS, BOTANIC GARDENS, DARWIN.

Photo, Ian Gilruth.

A WOOD-CART DRAWN BY A SOLEMN BLACK BUFFALO.

4 - Undercurrents

LIFE in Darwin is made up of many little worlds, each continuing in its own way, impinging on, but never mingling with the others. There is the life of white officialdom, the Eastern life of Chinatown, the life of the pearling fleets and, under all, the life of the native camps. A visitor may spend a week there, and the existence of these separate worlds may never dawn upon him. Or, again, in strolling along the beach, he may, in the space of a few moments, alight upon their outward signs. First he may walk into a party of blacks crooning soft corroboree songs to themselves; then he may suddenly come upon a small joss-house guarded by chipped stone dragons, with its gaudy gilt fretwork, waxen Images, and pewter bowls, glimmering through the incense-thickened air; and, looking out to sea, his eye may light on a fleet of pearling luggers, sailing lazily home like a flock of tired birds against a sunset sky.

Of all these aspects of life, perhaps that of the pearling fleet is the most apart, the most self-contained. The fleets arc owned by white men and worked by Japanese. As the law allows only a limited number of these to be indented they have matters more or less in their own hands, and can practically demand what conditions they please. At other pearling stations, such as those in the Duteh East Indics, the owner of the fleet, or some white man to represent him, travels with the boats in a schooner. Instead of going into port, the luggers get their supplies from this schooner, and also deliver over to it their catch. The shell is opened on board the schooner itself, and any lugger on which an open shell is found is subject to a fine. As shells open of themselves if they arc exposed for any length of time, this means that the luggers must come daily to the schooner, and thus the pearls fall directly into the hands of the master. In Darwin it is otherwise. The Japanese there refuse to work on this system, preferring to stay out a few weeks at a time, and then return to Darwin, where they hand over their shell, and "tucker up," as pro¬visioning is called. In consequence, the owners there seldom get possession of the pearls that arc rightly theirs, although they offer high rewards to any man who will bring them in. No reward seems to tempt the men, who prefer to get rid of their stolen property by more illicit means. The owners therefore make their entire profit out of the shell.

The life of the pearler is not an unhappy one. There is, of course, the risk of death, or-still more common-of paralysis, which very frequently overtakes the diver after some years. To make up for this, the work is not heavy and the wages are high. The diver is paid according to the weight of his catch, while each of the other men earns from £5 to £6 a month, and provisions are free. There are five men on each lugger - the diver, the tender, who manages the life-lines, and' three others to help work the ship, one of whom is generally training to become a diver himself. Their food and other supplies consist of rice, flour, dripping, jam, kerosene, candles, tea, coffee, and hops. Work stops during the very wet and stormy months, during which, as the law forbids them to be employed at anything else, they spend the time painting the boats. To add zest to ... their life, there is intense rivalry between the divers, each one endeavouring to outdo the others in the amount of shell his lugger brings back.

One morning we strolled along the foreshore, to witness the owner of a pearling fleet weighing each man's catch. The luggers were lying, sails furled, close in among the mangroves, their slender masts sending long quivering reflections through the still water. On their decks one or two short squat figures moved about, hanging up clothes to dry, or spreading red blankets over the side. In the foreground, one little brown man punted about lazily in a boat.

The divers from the luggers were collected in a group on the beach near by, where a weighing machine was planted on the stones. Beside it stood the owner of the fleet, "the Captain," clad in white from head to foot, holding a note-book and pencil. As we approached, two of the men piled on to the machine a mass of pearl shell - onc lugger's catch for six weeks. The owner eyed it carefully. Twice he stooped and picked out a shell whose surface was dull and worn. "Dead shell," he explained, "so it's no use to me and adds to the weight." When the pile was ready he prepared to weigh it, and suddenly the laughter and chatter ceased. The men crowded up round the machine and gazed breathlessly with bright, dark eyes, as the master carefully selected his weights. Thcy were a sturdy crew, short and square of figure, but not ill-looking. Some had an aristocratic curve of nose and line of olive cheek; others, more plebeian, had flat noses, short bristling hair above low foreheads, and skins pitted with smallpox. There Was an intense moment of waiting; then the Captain said calmly, "*The Esmeralda,* 9 cwt. 2 quarters, 13 lbs.," the tension relaxed, faces broke up into laughter again, and the chaff and chatter recommenced. The diver of the *Esmeralda* allowed himself a proud smile - as well he might, for he had cleared £14, and so far was well ahead of the other boats.

From the machine the shell was hurled with a clatter on to a great heap of stuff already weighed at one side. Here two dark morose Manila men were working silently, sorting it into sizes with marvellous rapidity and packing it into cases. The divers now prepared to pile the next load on to the weighing machine, but, before they could do so, there was a shout from the Captain of "Bag, bag!" Amid much laughter, they seized an old bag, and swept the machine free of the debris from the last lot, which wou1d have added to the weight, It was a perfectly good-natured warfare between master and men. The men's object was to cheat him if possible into weighing, and therefore paying for, what was really not of value; he naturally tried his best to circumvent them. The men's game was to forget each time to sweep the machine; the master's to keep a sharp look-out for dead shell, and never to forget the cry of " Bag!" And so the warfare went on, amidst endless jokes and merrimcnt, while to one side the two gloomy Manila men nailed down the cases that would not be opened again until they reached England or America.

A row of neat pearl buttons on a card - how commonplace, how quietly domestic they are! Nothing could appear more uninteresting than the material of which they are made, yet through what strange scenes of romance it has passed - calling men from sleepy Eastern villages, gathering them together in far-off countries, there to sail upon uncharted seas, to walk the bottom of the ocean, to laugh, to fight. to cheat, and perhaps to die.

Another industry of the Territory is the collection of tortoise-shell, though this is not carried on so systematically or on so large a scale as the pearling. Only one or two men engage in it, the chief of these being Joe Cooper, the buffalo hunter who dwells on Melville Island, forty miles from Darwin, the only white man among hundreds of savages. Sometimes a strange lugger, not belonging to any of the pearling fleets, enters the harbour and shelters in the cove of Lamaroo Beach, just below the town. This is Joe Cooper's craft, the *Buffalo*, which has brought over to Darwin its freight of horns and hides and tortoise-shell. Joe Cooper himself, big, bare-footed, loosely built, is to be seen strolling through the town, followed by six Melville Island natives, stepping proudly, bearing wide, black buffalo horns upon their shoulders.

On one visit the Buffalo had as its cargo three live turtles, which we were invited to see on Lamaroo Beach. We scrambled down the rough path of rock steps that descends the cliff through thick greenery to the beach below, where some blacks were camped. The old men glowered at us, some of the lubras grinned and nodded over their pipes, one or two children skipped round us im-pishly, but for the most part they were too much interested in the turtles to spare us any attention. Not far out, the lugger was swaying lazily on the blue water, while her black crew were on shore, chattering and giggling round the gigantic turtles. At a command from their master in their own language, they lifted the great yellow bulks, and carried them away from the edge of the water. The turtles raised their heads and an expression of piteous woe passed over their faces, which had an uncanny human cast, like those of fat, dull old gentlemen. They had no means of resisting the indignity of the proceeding, and seemed altogether stupefied, as if they had outlived some prehistoric age, which had rolled away and left them helpless in a bewildering new world. With slow, patient sweeps they made their way down to the sea, only to be brought back by the laughing blacks. One of these jumped on the back of the biggest of the three, unconsciously bearing partial testimony to the truth of De Rougemont's much disputed story.

These turtles were of the large edible kind, whose shell is of no value. It is the smaller, inedible turtle whose back polishes to the

THE LUGGERS WERE LYING, SAILS FURLED, CLOSE IN AMONG THE MANGROVES.

Photo, Mrs. Gilruth.

THE DIVERS FROM THE LUGGERS WERE A STURDY CREW.

brilliant black and yellow we know. Most of the shell that is collected in the Territory is scnt in its rough state to London, there to be made ready for market. There is one man, however, the keeper of the lighthouse at Point Charles that guards the entrance of Darwin harbour, who practises the art himself, catches his own turtles, polishes their shell and - cuts it into combs and ornaments.

We visited the lighthouse one day, puffing along the harbour in an oil-boat, steered by an old Malay with humorous, wrinkled face and far-seeing eyes. The little bay where the lighthouse stood recalled an old-fashioned woodcut in the Swiss Family Robinson. There were the low cliffs, the group of cocoanut palms above, sheltering two or three bark huts, a few natives on the beach, and one stalwart black paddling about amongst the rocks in a canoe. Only the big red and white lighthouse did not quite fit in to the picture; even the ingenious Robinson family could hardly have achieved that on their tropic isle.

We climbed the cliff, and went into the little galvanised iron house where one of the lighthouse men lives and keeps his curios. The room and verandahs were littered with huge" bailer" shells, lumps of coral, buffalo horns, tortoise-shell, rough and polished, and stuffed turtles. Behind the lighthouse stretched a neatly laid-out fruit garden, with rows of purpling pine-apple plants, bananas and lime trees laden with fruit. So, with the garden to look after, their craft to ply and the lamp to tend, it seemed the keepers of the Point Charles lighthouse would have little time to be lonely.

The industry of tortoise-shelling, like many others in the Territory, relies much for its labour on the natives. Indeed, the longer the visitor remains in the Territory, the more claims are made upon his attention by the blackfellow, the more interested does he become in that lowest of all the little worlds of Darwin - the world of native life. It flows on like an undercurrent, now rushing, now dwindling, but once its low note has struck the ear, it can never again be lost. Just in the same way, below the curious sounds that arise at night, drones the deep buzzing of the corrunbuek, the hollow bamboo pipe which accompanies the chant of a corroboree. Sometimes the corroboree breaks out louder and more insistent, when some party of aboriginals from the bush, perhaps from the Alligator River, from Daly Waters or

Borroloola, many miles away on the Gulf of Carpentaria, have come to Darwin. Possibly one has been brought in by the police as witness in some Court case, and has been accompanied by family and friends. Or it may be that five or six have wandered in of their own accord to live a life of semi-civilisation and to know the luxury of blankets, tobacco, and plenty of tucker.

On one occasion such a party came to Darwin from Borroloola, and made their camp at the back of the police station, on what was at one time the concrete foundation of a house which was blown down in the great cyclone. Here not only they, but also all the Borroloola natives who were already in Darwin would collect when the day's work was over. Every night, as soon as darkness fell, the regular beating of sticks and clapping of hands from behind the police station announced that the corroboree had begun. On the third night the clapping was more insistent than ever; at last a snatch of chant, wafted over to us by the breeze, proved irresistible. We made our way across the road to a stretch of common ground, pushed aside the prickly branches of sweet-smelling horehound, and found ourselves at the scene of a corroboree.

A ring of dark crouching forms sat round the concrete, each beside a small fire of glowing embers. In the centre of the concrete, which shone a blank white in the moonlight, five or six wild figures stamped and gesticulated, while one man squatted on the ground before them, clapping two boomerangs together and singing his harsh song. The chant began high up and wandered restlessly about like a strayed ghost seeking its grave, until at last it fell contented to a low growl, so deep that it was hardly a note at all. "Wanee, wanee, wanee-maa," cried the singer in a high-pitched quaver - "Wanee-maa. Moree, moree, langobaa." At last it began to sink, but no, up it rose once more. "Moree, moree, wanee-rnaa " - and now at last it settled down to the long last nasal "langobaa." With what strange sadness that chant was burdened! The desolate melancholy of desert places, the mystery of dark, swirling rivers, the cries of birds and beasts in the primeval bush, all the struggle for life of this lonely people in a vast land seemed to find voice in the wild minor cadence.

The dancers had meanwhile been advancing towards the singer, bounding stiffly, their knees and feet turned outwards, their bodies held rigid. Faster and faster they came, hissing excitedly between their teeth. Then, as the song came to a sudden end, they too stopped dead, stamped their hard feet on the hard concrete, and shouted hoarsely, waving their arms, "Birrilalaa, Birrilalaa." A pause, while only the boomerangs tapped, and then the wild outbreak of the chant once more.

Perhaps they were describing their journey from Borroloola - Birrilalaa - to Darwin; perhaps they were enacting some far older drama. We could get no satisfactory answers to our questions. Every now and then one of the dancers would tire and flop down on the ground for a smoke. There would be the scratch of a match, and a sudden flare lighting a shining black face. But the numbers of performers never decreased, for marc and more natives, like long dark shadows in the moonlight, came silently wandering up to the corroboree ground, approaching so noiselessly on their bare feet that they seemed to have suddenly risen out of the earth.

The next performance was the imitation of a horse. Five of them crouched in line, holding one to the other, and pranced up the concrete. Then with one accord they all shied violently, dashing away to the side with a terrified whinny. This was received by the lubras with shrieks of discordant laughter, the only addition they made to the evening's entertainment. One lubra, however, seemed too busy even to laugh. She sat close up to her fire, bending intently over something, which turned out to be a bag she was making of dirty white calico. Beside her lay a dilly-bag of the old pattern, made of human hair and dyed red and blue, but this she pushed aside with contempt. "Makem new fella," she declared, proudly showing her handiwork. Her thread, which was immensely long, invariably got entangled in her black toes, and had to be unwound between every stitch, so that the making of the bag promised to be a long affair. But, after all, whether it was finished next day, next month, next year - what did it matter to her?

This lubra, Nellie, was an object of interest to us, for her husband Sambo had just returned from a trip to the south-unwanted experience for a blackfellow.

"Sambo dere," she answered, with a delighted chuckle. " Sambo come back longa me. That one too muchee cold country."

" You likem Melbourne?" we asked of the lanky Sambo.

"My word, Missis, me likem orright. Me ride longa train, longa tramcar, longa motor car." He paused, and then, with the air of a connoisseur in cities, "Melbourne him good fella; Sydney good fella. Brisbane no good." In what the capital of Queensland fell short we never heard, for at that moment the corroboree became too much for Sambo and he dashed into the dance.

We left the corroboree ground, and the tapping and chanting grew gradually fainter behind us. Finally it died away altogether, drowned by the sound of a neighbouring piano and the strident strains of a gramophone - prophetic, so it seemed to us, of the fate of this primitive people, relic of a bygone era.

BLACKS AT CORROBOREE

5 - OUT BUSH

THE first part of a journey "out bush " in the Northern Territory is generally taken in the train, just as it might be in more civilised countries. Yet this particular train is of peculiar interest, for it is the pioneer on what will one day be the Great Australian Overland Route. It seems to have a special personality of its own. It is a plucky, fussy little train, full of self-importance, as it starts out twice a week on its journey of a hundred and forty-seven miles to Pine Creek. Every Monday and Thursday at eight o'clock in the morning, it stands all ready at the station, where its departure is awaited by a crowd of light-suited and helmeted white men, agitated Chinese clasping shiny baskets and large blue umbrellas, and black - boys with parcels and letters for the country mail. The train gives an impatient shriek which seems to say, " Come along, come along, there'll be the deuce to pay if I'm not in Pine Creek by half-past four this afternoon," the passengers swing on board, and it trots out.

To old bushmen who have travelled many times in this same train since first the railway was built there is no interest in the passing scenery. But to the traveller to whom the Northern Territory is still new it is impossible to spend the eight hours' journey yarning inside the carriage, when with every second he is speeding away towards the centre of Australia. Far better he finds it to stand on the little platform beside the swinging water-bag and watch the strange, new bush, so familiar in some ways, so curiously foreign in others. The train rushes through stretches of forest, lightly timbered with gum-trees, fresh, green Leichardt pines, cycad palms, and bright flowering kapok. In the wet season the country is a brilliant green, and kangaroo and wallaby dash away from each side of the line; in the dry months the grass is long and golden and animal life much scarcer. All through the bush stand great ant-hills like rough-hewn turrets of red and grey. There is something strangely impressive about the giant ant-hill, something solemn and primeval in its huge, castellated bulk. Standing lonely and indifferent among the trees, it has a dignity and rough beauty of its own that no man-made masonry can surpass. Sometimes there is an out-crop of the meridional kind, built with sharp flanges, whieh always mysteriously point north and south.

Every now and then comes a patch of " debbil-debbil " country, sandy soil, churned up by the rains in the wet season and in the dry months nothing but ruts and tussocks, sparsely grassed and scattered with a few clumps of pandanus, Next, the train stops for a drink at the Darwin River, deep, green, and mysterious, overhung by palms and drooping paper-bark; then it rushes on again refreshed, pounding away furiously, gasping for breath and altogether making as much fuss as if it were doing a hundred miles an hour instead of twenty.

The moving spirit of the train is" George." George leaves Darwin a railway guard in a regulation peaked cap, but before he reaches the Four Mile, he changes his cap for an old felt hat and becomes to the passengers one of themselves. Every now and then he pops a smiling sunburnt face in at the door, waves a bottle of soda-water chilled in his freezer, and shouts cheerily, "Like a drink? " He stops a moment to tell a yarn of the old days when the railway train was sowing its wild oats, then, as it draws up before the solitary cottage of a ganger, he is off to unload tanks of water or timber from a truck, hand out letters and parcels and exchange news with the ganger's wife. There is one of these small cottages every ten miles or so along the line, built of corrugated iron with bougainvillea creeper covering the verandah, a few banana palms and paw-paw trees growing at the back and a flock of white goats feeding near. It is no use asking for a name by which to call these little stations. Even George fails here, and can only tell you that it is the Ten Mile, the Twenty-two-and-a-Half Mile, or the Hundred-and-Four Mile. When it is suggested that it might be convenient to name them, he answers cheerfully, "What's the use? What d'you want to call them anything for? Everybody knows them."

At one point the train probably passes the gangers themselves working on the line. Their mail is passed out attached to a hoop of wire, and one shouts, "George, tell Bill at the Eighty-eight I've got his knife all right." "Right oh! " calls George, who has already a dozen such messages to remember.

The first long pause is at the Adelaide River, where Widgee, a fat, jolly, half-caste woman provides hot water for luncheon tea, an old

Chinaman with a buffalo cart brings paw-paw and water-melon to sell at the train, and a troop of blacks in bright-red turkey twill march swiftly along the line, on the look-out for tucker.

The only township on the way is Brock's Creek. In the old days, when the English company was exploiting the mines of the Territory, Brook's Creek was a populated place. Mineral was there, but, owing to various reasons, the mines failed and Brook's Creek lost its importance. Many of its buildings were carted away to be set up elsewhere, leaving only a hotel, a school, one or two houses, and a Chinatown. Except for one enterprising couple who are extracting ore from old sand heaps by means of the cyanide process, and a few patiently fossicking Chinese, the mining at Brock's Creek is a thing of the past. But it may not always be so. Before long doubtless Brock's Creek will be once more a lively mining township. In the meantime it is still of importance, for a road leads out from there over a ridge of blue hills to the great Daly River where a Government Experiment now flourishes and new settlers are taking up land.

After Brock's Creek the country becomes more hilly, and stony ridges scarred with deserted mines close in round the line. The train gives its final shriek, puts on an extra spurt, and pounds into Pine Creek.

The traveller who has looked out Pine Creek on the map and sees its name printed in type as large as that of Sydney or Melbourne, experiences a slight shock when he alights there. For Pine Creek consists only of a line of iron and wooden buildings straggling down one side of a street. It has, nevertheless, its hospital, two hotels, one or two stores, a school, and the dwellings of white officials such as the Protector of Aboriginals, and the Police. Beyond the township is a low range, riddled with old mining shafts, and behind this lie the brushwood roofs and drooping flagstaffs of Chinatown, Beyond, the Overland Telegraph leads on southwards into the alluring purple distance.

As the traveller strolls down the one street in the soft glow of the evening sun, his imagination flies forward to the time when Pine Creek will be an important station on the overland route, when the train will bear on board all the English mails from the south and will have no time to dawdle on the way. Then it will be crowded with tourists taking the quickest route to the old world *via* Darwin and the east, only perfunctorily interested when they are told they are passing through the great Northern Territory, famous for its pastoral lands, its agriculture, its mining-and openly bored with the old pioneer who insists on forcing on them his reminiscences of the early days of the Northern Territory.

Next day, the little train faces eastwards once more and runs back the hundred and forty-seven miles to Darwin. From Pine Creek the traveller goes by coach to the Katherine, the next station on the Overland Telegraph, and now he is well into the Never-Never, where his chance of reaching his destination depends solely on his horses, his black-boys, and himself. So he prepares to pack his swag and set off on the long trek, knowing that he will thus experience to the full the fascinations of the Northern Territory bush.

If he were starting on a similar journey in southern Australia he could nearly always rely on finding ahead of him good roads and fairly good hotels. Here he cannot count on anything of the sort. He may eventually arrive at an out-back station, but he knows that before doing so he must pass many nights camping far away from other white men. Therefore everything he needs he must carry with him. Yet, as the fewer pack-horses he takes the faster he will travel, one of the first considerations is to reduce the baggage as much as possible.

Each man's luggage consists of a single swag. The outside of this consists of a big canvas sheet, which is rolled round the parts of a collapsible stretcher, a bush mosquito net made of cheese-cloth with a calico top, rugs, a quart pot, and a change of clothes. The provisions are of the simplest-corned beef, flour for damper, tea and sugar. These are tied up in bags of unbleached calico, which can be hung on trees in camp and thus prevent the ants from reaching the food. With bare necessities in the way of knives, forks, spoons, enamel plates, a billy, a tomahawk, guns and ammunition, and possibly in addition a few luxuries in the way of tinned meats, fruit, jam, milk, and butter, the expedition is equipped.

Day begins early in camp. With the first grey. glimmer of dawn comes a long cry of "Dayli-ight." There is a moment's silence and then everyone creeps out from under the mosquito nets and sets about the morning duties - lighting the fire, shaking the dew from the nets, rolling swags, and making breakfast. Long before the awaken¬ing of camp the black-boy has stolen away after the pack-horses, which have wandered far during the night, and soon they all come crashing into camp. The hobbles are taken off and knotted round the horses' necks, packs are loaded (first being carefully weighed to make sure they balance), and by the time the sun is over the top of the trees the party is on the march.

The bush travellers make a picturesque cavalcade. Ahead ride the white men, at a swift steady walk of three-and-a-half miles an hour; behind, the pack - horses come shambling along, driven by the blue-shirted, felt-hatted black-boys. They jig on contentedly, sitting well back in the saddle, knees jammed under the pads, elbows out, reins held high, until a pack-horse strays from the track, when, uttering shrill whoops, they dash after it among the trees. The track, which may be well defined with the wheel-marks of last year's wagons, or may be only a bridle-pad, leads through wooded country, over long stretches of sand, plains of "debbil-debbil" country, and occasionally to a creek flowing between banks of soft feathery bamboo and other shady jungle trees. In the dry season there is no difficulty in crossing; the black-boys urge on the packhorses, and, amid much whip - cracking, shouting, splashing, and trampling, they are steered safely down the bank and up the other side. As the day gets warmer, the bush becomes hushed and lifeless. When the first convenient water is reached there is a halt for the noon-day rest and meal. Everyone feels silent and drowsy, the gumleaves hang listlessly from, the branches; there is not the flutter of a bird in the trees, not the stir of an animal in the long grass. Towards evening, as the shadows lengthen, and the late sunlight, slanting through the trees, seems to diffuse the hush with gold dust, life begins to move again, and all the wild things come out to feed. Now is the chance for a shot - at a grey kangaroo sitting up to gaze, motionless as a stump, or, if water is near, at a wild turkey or goose.

Camp is pitched for the night on the banks of a creek or a water-hole. First the packs are unloaded and the horses taken to bathe and drink at the farther end of the water. Then they are hobbled and set free to feed. While this is being done, one man lights the fire, mixes the damper of flour and water and covers it over with the hot ashes. This is to-morrow's damper, for it takes too long to cook to be ready for dinner that night. Meanwhile the swags are unrolled and the beds made ready. In the wet season it is as well to use a stretcher, for the ground is damp and there is a risk of snakes and other crawling things. But in the dry, when the nights are bitterly cold, it is better to make one's bed on the ground, so that the chilly air does not strike up from below. First a hip hole is dug out, then grass, collected by the black-boys, is laid on the hearth, on top of that the camp sheet, and then rugs, as many as can be carried in the swag. Over it all the mosquito net is slung, tied to trees or to stakes. The quart pots are then ranged round the fire, and, by the time the sun sets, dinner is ready.

With darkness, especially in the coastal districts, come the mosquitoes; so, after tomorrow's plans have been discussed, every one goes off to bed. There is nothing more delicious than a night in camp. The soul of the bush seems to be breathed out in the fragrant scents of roots, earth and trees. You wake to hear the gentle tinkle of horse bells, rustling of birds and beasts, the whistling wail of curlews, and the black boys round the fire exchanging guttural words. Towards morning it becomes unbearably cold, and there is a general movement of campers turning and rolling themselves tighter in their rugs. Then silence, until the cry of " Daylight" wakes them to another day's trek.

But such pleasant journeying is only possible in well-watered country. Towards the end of the rainless months, in some of the inland districts, there are long dry stages, when the traveller rides at night, urging his thirsty, tired horses from one water to another, and camps during the heat of the day. Sometimes even when water is at last reached it is muddy and evil-smelling. The tale is told of two travellers who asked of a chance man they met if the next water were good. "It's A1," was the answer; "there's two dead bullocks in it, but they won't be bust before you get there."

These chance meetings are not frequent, but sometimes on the road one comes on a solitary man-a miner, a carter or a stockman. Although he may not have seen another white man for many months, he shows no curiosity, no surprise, no emotion of any kind. He squats down on his heels, lights his pipe, and so remains until it is time to move on again. The only two subjects of discussion are grass and water, but there is no outpouring of talk. His tongue has grown rusty in solitude. When he tries to give directions and information, his speech is slow, full of reiteration and hesitation, and it is clear that the process of translating thoughts into words is painful to him. Next day he takes up his lonely journey without regret, yet that meeting has been one of the events of his life, every detail of which, every chance word uttered by the strangers, is treasured in a store of memories destined never to be expressed. At last the station homestead is sighted - a corrugated iron building standing in a cleared patch, with a few banana trees in front and a vegetable garden not far off. The approach of the travellers arouses great commotion. Blacks rush towards the house, calling the news shrilly, their dogs yap, an excited Chinese cook runs out from the back, fowls cluck and scatter, and the boss himself appears to wave a welcome.

There is a rough verandah outside the building where harness and water-bags hang. Inside it is divided into three by iron partitions. The main room has a table with sauces, bottles of "square" and a tin or two upon it; there is a pile of old newspapers in one corner, rifles and guns in another. The storeroom contains all the flour, tea and tinned provisions which are to last till the wagons next come out, and also cotton dresses, shirts, pipes, tobacco and beads for the blacks.

At the back an open . shed, with a fireplace and planks for shelves, serves the Chinese cook as kitchen and pantry. It is very different, however, if there is a woman on the place. Then there is a proper kitchen, cupboards, however rough, for household goods, and everywhere signs of an endeavour to make the place a home, not merely a temporary shelter between camps. There is no difficulty in accommodating the travellers, for it is an understood thing that they set up their own camp somewhere near the house. They are made very welcome for the evening meal, and they revel in station fare-fresh milk, vegetables and bread. In return, they deliver a mail and recount the news - what is doing in Darwin; if So-and-So, who was on trial for cattle-stealing, has got off; whether the Roper River police got that blackfellow who was wanted; and endless details about this man's horses and that man's cattle. Every incident of the journey, every water-hole, is discussed, and it is late when the last pipe is smoked and the last good-nights arc said.

PINE CREEK.

Photo, Professor Baldwin Spencer.

THE MOTOR-CAR IN THE BUSH.

6 - BY MOTOR-CAR TO UMINDIDU

WITHIN the last two years the experiment has been made of travelling through the bush of the Northern Territory in a motor-car instead of by horse. It was a bold experiment in a country roadless, sometimes for long stretches waterless, and sparsely populated. Each time a journey has been done there have been many difficulties with tyres or petrol or water. There has been much discomfort and the travellers have had to work with pick and shovel and to walk long distances under a blazing sun. A motor journey through the Northern Territory is never undertaken for pleasure, but solely for the purpose of traversing the country in as short a. time as possible.

The motor-car that first undertook these long bush journeys was the object of much talk and criticism, on its arrival, from those who held that horses were the only possible means of transport in the Territory, and that it was madness to attempt to drive a motor through the bush. The car was a 15 horse-power Colonial Napier, and it caused much excitement in Darwin. One other had been seen there some years previously, but this was the first to many of the population. Little groups of whites, blacks, and yellows collected at street corners to gaze, horses snorted with indignation, and the Chinaman's buffaloes rolled resentful eyes.

With the car arrived the chauffeur on whose skill and resource the success of the experiment so much depended. After the manner of chauffeurs he worshipped the car above all mundane things, while the car's master served as a minor deity. Moreover, he possessed that necessary attribute of the chauffeur - he inspired confidence, and before long he had shown that he fully deserved it.

After a few short drives about Darwin a trial trip was decided upon to find out whether the car were fit for bush service.

Umdidu (Humpty Doo), a station forty-one miles from Darwin and only twenty from the railway line, was chosen as suitable for a day's run. The car was loaded up with some provisions, two planks, in case it encountered sandy ground, and a tomahawk. Old residents shook their heads over the dangers of the trip, and bets were made against the chances of the car and its occupants getting back to Darwin the same day. It was a determined party and a still more determined chauffeur that set out that morning at 7.30 for Umdidu.

The first part of the way was easy going, although "down below" it would hardly have been called a good road. We tooted gaily past the Railway Works at the Two and-a-Half Mile, and were soon in the typical Northern Territory bush with its outstanding features of gum-trees, ant-hills, kangaroos and wallabies. The car should have been satisfied with the sensation she caused amongst the wild game. They were fairly well accustomed to the railway train, but what new monster was this which, instead of keeping to a defined track, actually plunged right into the bush? They flew rather than jumped across our path and dashed away into the scrub.

Presently we emerged on a Chinaman's grey bark hut, with a few banana palms waving round it, and then drew up before the white cottages of the gangers who live at the Ten Mile. Here there were some black-boys with pack-horses who were also setting out for the Twenty Mile, but they were following the railway, whereas we were going by road. Everything that can travel along the line does so, and only wagons have still to follow the old road through the bush. But no wagons had journeyed from the Ten to the Twenty Mile for six years, and six successive wet seasons are quite enough to wipe out all signs of a track underfoot; though, if you look carefully, you can pick out a faint line where there are no very big trees. Sometimes it jumps to the eye, but, if you once let your gaze wander, it is gone and seems lost for ever.

Very soon our chauffeur had gained our admiration by his splendid driving. But even his readiness could not quite save us, and we ricocheted from ant-hill to rock, from rock to tree, while deceptive stumps embowered in green ripped at the motor, and six-year-old saplings crashed down before us. Our chauffeur remained as calm as if he were tooling along Piccadilly, and after some hair-raising manoeuvring, "Which way, sir?" he would say to the leader of the party, who sat leaning forward, his eyes fixed, pointing out the road. Sometimes we managed to dodge logs; at other times, when going to one side meant striking an ant-hill, we had to chop them away with a tomahawk. The chauffeur soon became expert in knowing which of the young trees were too big to tackle, and which we could safely ride over; he aimed accurately at these with the centre of the radiator, and down they went, springing up again after we had passed, a-quiver with indignation.

We lost our axle-stay and presently - far more serious - we lost our road. It happened in this way. First we passed through a forest of Leichardt pines, pretty trees with broad smooth leaves of a light fresh green; then we plunged down into a dry creek bed; up the other side, and lo! the road was gone! It had wandered off into a patch of devil-devil country, nothing but little lumps of sand, and only sparsely scattered with pandanus palms, so that we could no longer follow the line where the big trees had been cut down. Faint tracks of the wagons ran out into the grey sand and then vanished utterly.

For over an hour we looked for that road, climbing little rocky hillocks, following wallaby tracks, plunging into jungly creek beds, retracing our way and always returning to where the big grey car sat in mid-bush, incongruous and unconcerned. From the little rises we could see nothing but waving green tree-tops; no change, no landmark in any direction. It would be fatally easy to get lost in this country, to wander for days without water, knowing that it was possibly within a few yards all the time.

We were all scattered in different directions, hopefully following up tracks of game, only to find them disappear into the sand, when a sudden cooee from our leader announced that the road was found. He had returned again and again to a water-hole; and, starting out from there, had caught at last the faint tracks of the wagons. So the car jolted across the "debbil-debbil" and was soon crashing and bumping through the bush as before. After that we all became more expert in picking out the road and in descrying the wicked little stumps that tried to hide themselves in greenery. At last we hailed with joy the glimmer of the Twenty Mile Shed through the trees, and after a final wild plunge through bush, came out on the railway line, to the astonishment of two gangers who were working there.

From the railway, we dashed off along the road that leads to Umdidu. This time it really was a road, clean and smooth, and the car raced on to make up for the previous delays. It was already past one o'clock, so we stopped for lunch at the first water, a little billabong covered with white waterlilies. It was only then, when no longer the breeze caused by the rush of the car fanned our faces, that we noticed how the great heat of the day had crept upon us. The bush lay motionless under the burning sun, a rest for the sake of our chauffeur, to relieve for a few moments the strain on his arms and eyes. He, on the other hand, was only eager to water his beloved car.

Lunch over, we whirled once more along the road, flashing past shaded water-holes, past groups of slate-blue meridional anthills, until we suddenly turned a bend and ran into another big patch of "debbil-debbil." The road became nothing but sand; the engine made one violent effort to wrench the car free, but in vain; she sank up to the axle and stopped dead. We tried a hauling tackle, which proved a failure, and planks which were no better, and we were just casting about to find what to do next, when there suddenly appeared over the horizon a little clump of horses and riders. They came shambling rapidly towards us and turned out to be two white men and a black boy with their pack-horses. They were immediately hailed with a shout of "Come and push!"

Down they got and joined the other two men at the back of the car; then five pairs of shoulders made one big heave all together, and the car was lifted on to the planks. After that we exchanged greetings and news; then we waved good-bye, and the little cavalcade set off once more for the railway. It was train day; they were to catch the train at the Twenty Mile, so we knew that the tale of our having been stuck in the sand would be in Darwin before us and would increase the odds against our return that night.

For a while we journeyed on without mishap. Then we struck an unavoidable stump with such a crash that we thought all the vital part of the car must have been ripped out. But our driver said calmly, "It's only the engine cover," and we went on, leaving a large battered piece of metal lying by the roadside.

The next contretemps was at a creek that flowed through a belt of cool dark jungle, where tall white-stemmed palms shot up to the sky, and great trees, all wound about by snaky creepers, shut out the light - alas, where mosquitoes made the air thick and leeches waved about hungrily on the leaves at our feet. The creek was muddy and sluggish, and there was no way to reach the other side except to make a dash through. The dash came to a standstill in the middle, and the car settled down comfortably into the mud. This time it seemed hopeless, so we two women crossed the creek on planks and started to walk in to Umdidu to get help, leaving the men to work at the car. We would have done better to have waited in the shade trusting to our chauffeur; for, after we had walked for an hour and still there was no sign of the homestead, there was a cheery "toot-toot" behind us, and up came the car. I will not attempt to explain by what miracle - working the chauffeur had extricated her.

Only a few minutes more, and we emerged on the open plain, where stands the picturesque homestead of Umdidu - two iron buildings in a small enclosure which contained a few banana palms and a haystack. As we approached, an agitated old Chinaman, a fat lubra, several cattle dogs and some fowls ran out to greet us. Ah Toy explained that the Boss was away, gone to bring in a man who had been gored through the foot; and then he disappeared at the back of the house to make us some tea.

Umdidu was a typical station homestead with its verandah a litter of harness, waterbags, mosquito netting, tools, and its rooms mere partitions divided by iron walls, with floors formed of logs cut in cross-sections and embedded in earth. The store-room stood open to the world, and the kitchen was only a camp fire, roughly sheltered by a piece of corrugated iron.

Ah 'I'oy soon bustled back with the tea and a jug of goats' milk - a cheery, flurried little soul, desperately anxious to do whatever might be required of him. And a good deal besides the making of meals is required of a station cook. It is said that on one occasion a visitor heard the Boss abusing Ah Toy for some duty undone, and ventured to take the little Chinaman's part, declaring that he was really a very good cook, to which his master shouted in reply: "Cook! What's the good to me of a cook that can only cook? I want one that can drive in posts."

We left Umdidu before five o'clock, crossed the difficult creek by means of planks, picked up the engine-cover, skirted the sand, and arrived back at the railway line at half-past six, just as the sun was setting. Darkness descends almost immediately after sun-. set in these parts, and we realised that to attempt the so-called road between the Twenty and the Ten Mile would mean spending the night in the bush for certain. There was nothing for it but to try the railway line. "We knew that we should have trouble with the bridges, of which there is one every mile or so. These pass over steep- banked beds of creeks, dry during the winter months, but where torrents run in the wet season. They arc of the scantiest construction - the rails running across wooden sleepers, laid very wide apart without ballast.

There was no way of going round them; all that could be done was to drive straight over, and after we had tackled the first we saw what a serious business it was going to be. The car bumped wildly over the iron pins that supported the rails, the wheels fitting just outside them, and having only two or three inches to spare on either side, so that a swerve would have sent us hurtling over the edge. When we came to the second bridge, the chauffeur insisted that we should get out, partly to avoid risk and partly to lighten the motor. We walked on in advance, and then turned to see the car slowly crawling across the bridge. There was a creepy fascination in watching those headlights waving up and down, stopping, then waving again to the accompaniment of a loud jarring from engine and brakes. Every mile or so the same thing had to be gone through, but the plucky chauffeur sat imperturbable at his wheel, though it was touch - and - go each time. At last the inevitable happened. On a small bridge at the Sixteen Mile the hind-wheels became jammed between the sleepers. The men worked for half an hour with apparently no effect, and at last we women-folk decided to walk on to the Ten Mile and send back help. In spite of our anxiety for the rest of the party, and our own weariness, it was a delicious walk. Rich moonlight flooded everything; the air was fragrant with the pungent scents of the bush at night, and full of the scurryings and thumpings of wild things among the trees. Once we noticed a strong smell of cooking. "Come on," we said to each other, "there's the Ten Mile having its supper." But the smell passed, and we knew it must have come from a camp of blacks cooking their game and yams.

At last we saw what looked like a post and signboard ahead. Hastily one of us ran to look at it. It was indeed a post, and told us that we had reached the crossing just before the Ten Mile. "That post says, 'Look out for the train,'" we said, and then lay full length on the line, leaning our heads on the rail to rest. There are not many parts of the world left where one can thus safely defy railway boards. But the thought that the men were working hard to extricate the car spurred us on; in a few minutes we were round the bend and knocking at the door of the ganger's cottage, with the dogs of the Ten Mile barking at our heels. The men were already in bed, but they leaped up when they heard our story, and in a few minutes were rattling along the line on their trolley to the rescue of the motor. We sat on the verandah of the cottage drinking welcome cups of tea, and strained our ears for the first sounds of the car. For three-quarters of an hour we waited. Then we heard a terrific clattering, and saw the great head-lights bearing down upon us. From the noise we made sure that the engine must be in pieces; but it was due to quite another cause, for-triumph of triumphs - the car was towing back the trolley that had been sent out to rescue her.

The gangers had arrived just as the men of our party had managed to get her across the bridge. But they had got into fresh difficulties after we had left. The position in which we had last seen her was, in their own words, "a fool to the one she got into next"; for, in freeing the back wheels, she had got tightly jammed between the next two sleepers. However, by means of planks, by heaving, by working the engine, they had extricated her and crossed the bridge at last. The gang men were aghast at the feats of our chauffeur, and regarded him as a giant of pluck and encrgy - as indeed he was.

From the Ten Mile our way was clear. We ran swiftly through the moonlit bush, flashed past the Railway Works at the Two-and-a-Half Mile, and tooted through the streets of

Darwin at five minutes before midnight, Our backers had won their bets: the first experiment had succeeded, and the car had shown herself capable of coping with the wild bush ways of the Northern Territory.

SOMETIMES ONE COMES ON A SOLITARY MAN—A MINER, A CARTER, OR A STOCKMAN.

A LITTLE BILLABONG COVERED WITH WATER-LILIES.

7 - OENPELLI, A BUFFALO-HUNTER'S HOME

EVERY now and then, in out-of-the-way corners of the Northern Territory, one comes across the settlement-sometimes little more than a camp- of a buffalo hunter. Here he dwells in a hut made by his own hands, cooking his own rough meals, his only companions his horses and the natives of the district, whom he trains to hunt with him. The hunting party wanders far from the main camp, following the track of buffalo, until it comes in sight of a herd of the ponderous black beasts, with their sweeping horns, feeding on the long grass of the plains, resting in the shade of a clump of pandanus, or pushing their way through jungle to a water-hole to drink. Once they get wind of men, away they go, and with a shout the hunters set off after them, at a mad gallop in which only the most reckless rider can join. When they get near enough, they fire, aiming at the back-bones of the buffalo; and the horses are trained to spring away as soon as they hear the shot, so that they may avoid the fall of the wounded beast.

When the buffalo hunter has collected enough horns and hides, he brings them in to Darwin, perhaps overland by packhorse, or, if his camp is near the coast, in a lugger manned by blacks. Away go the hides on a steamer to the civilised world; away goes the buffalo hunter back to his lonely life in the bush.

Unwittingly each of these men does something towards opening up the country. Their journeys on horseback make a bridle track from the railway line to their camp, where before all was unknown bush. In the course of their hunting they explore wide tracts of land, follow rivers to their sources, accustom natives to the sight of white men, and by the time the buffaloes are all shot out and the hunter has gone to other parts, that little patch of the Territory has lost its remoteness.

Yet not all the hunters leave the country when their game has disappeared. Sometimes they settle on their old hunting-ground, make a home there, and turn their hands to other things. Such is the case with Paddy Cahill, the famous hunter of the Alligator River. Once large herds of buffalo roved over the wide, grassy plains that stretch away on either side of the stream, but now they only appear occasionally and in small numbers. Paddy Cahill, however, still lives on the Alligator, and acts as protector to the aborigines of the district. The banks of the river teem with wild-fowl, so the blacks have never lacked food, and are, in consequence, a fine race of strong, muscular men and pretty, plump lubras. No Chinese are settled there to demoralise them with grog and opium. Here is the Australian aboriginal unspoilt, morally and physically, and here, if anywhere, is the chance of civilising him successfully.

Paddy Cahill is beginning in the right way. The men are learning to grow vegetables and to build houses of simple design, the lubras are being trained in domestic work, and in due time a school will be established, where the children will be taught reading and writing. But the secret of Paddy Cahill's success lies in his unbounded influence over the natives and in his wonderful sympathy with their customs and beliefs. He never laughs at them; he speaks to them in their own language, and calls them by their native names. In return, they give him their confidence, and no ceremony is too sacred to be enacted before him. Those who work on the homestead are well cared for, induced to be clean, and doctored if they are ill. Their relations with Paddy Cahill are of the friendliest, and yet, though they laugh and joke together, there is never a tinge of insolence on the part of the blacks. You feel that here they have found a true friend and protector-one who, while not discarding their ways, will lead them gradually to his own.

Paddy Cahill's station, Oenpelli, is truly isolated. To the west his nearest neighbour is reached after a journey of four clays overland by horse, at Burrundie, a small siding on the railway line; to the east there is no one between him and the Arafura Sea. Every six weeks or so, Romula, a faithful black henchman, rides into Burrundie and back with mails, or else Paddy Cahill himself sails down the river in his lugger and round the coast to Darwin. This is in the dry season; in the wet, the track is often im-passable and storms make the sea journey dangerous, so that the dwellers at Oenpelli are sometimes for six months without a mail.

It was for this remote station that we set out one day in the little steamer *Stuart*, of 280 tons. Her ultimate destination was the Roper River in the Gulf of Carpentaria, but on the way she was to call at the East Alligator River, and to land on the banks, near Oenpelli, a party of surveyors who were to make the first survey of the country.

The *Stuart* left Darwin behind her one blazing noon, and started forth on her long cruise eastwards. She steamed past low-lying islands, through tropic seas, where occasionally the blunt head of a turtle appeared above the water, or a yellow-and-black water-snake was tossed past on the ripples, helpless as a banana skin. On the second day out she made her way towards a blank space in the close line of mangroves, the mouth of the Alligator River. Twelve miles up the river she dropped anchor, and the cruise was continued in a motor-boat towing a punt and a dinghy. We all hoped to find Oenpelli that night, but where to find it was another matter. We knew the station was not situated right on the banks of the river; but how far up it was, where to find the track that led to it, not one of the party had any idea. We pinned our faith to the information that " a fellow in Darwin" had given our commander. It seemed that Smith, a departed buffalo hunter, had once built a jetty in the stream, and that there we could pick up a friendly native who would show us the rest of the way.

"You just go round the bend," said the fellow in Darwin, "and there's Smith's jetty. You can't miss it." We went round the bend, and after that many more bends, and most certainly we missed it.

For miles and miles we saw nothing but mangroves, grey mud, wild-fowl, and alligators. The alligators, which lay sunning themselves on long spits of mud, were of all sizes, from a baby of two or three feet, like a gigantic lizard that wriggled wildly down the bank at our approach, to a huge twenty-foot monster that slowly launched himself into the river, lifted a wicked, grinning old face for an instant above the water, and then vanished swiftly and suddenly. It was eerie to look at the dull yellow surface of the stream, and think of those great scaly brutes silently pursuing their ways beneath its surface.

The wild-fowl swarmed. Cockatoos hung on the mangroves like large white blossoms; elegant cranes posed daintily on the grey mud; ducks and geese flew in wavy lines across the river; once a flock of turkeys flapped over our heads. But of human habitation the only trace we saw was one native dug-out canoe, lying empty close in to shore. Had we been the first explorers of that river - a boatload of sturdy red-faced Dutchmen, perhaps - with what apprehension we would have beheld that canoe; how sharp a look-out we would have kept for dark forms writhing their way through the mangrove roots; how we would have primed our muskets in readiness for a horde of savages descending upon us with spears and poisoned arrows. As it was, the one thing in the world we wanted to see was a blackfellow. None appeared. There was not even the smoke of a camp fire, and we saw gradually fade away our visions of a neatly-made pier running out into the water, and an eager native stepping down jauntily to offer his services.

At last there appeared ahead two fuzzy, cone-shaped hills, which, as we approached, turned out to be formed of big rocks piled on each other, with jungle growing in the clefts. There were two or three of these strange cones, scattered over a yellow plain, where a few pandanus palms grew in sketchy clumps. Here we stopped to reconnoitre, and lit upon a strange discovery. We climbed up a cleft between two rocks through a tangle of creeper, crawled on our hands and knees up a dark tunnel, with little bats softly hitting our faces, and emerged on a sunny platform, surrounded by great rocks and smelling sweetly of spinifex. The underside of one of these was covered with crude images in red, yellow, and white clay. It was a native picture gallery we had discovered. For the most part the paintings seemed to be of birds and fishes, but here and there was an unmistakable alligator or a human form; and scattered amongst them all was the imprint of a red hand. We longed for someone learned in black lore to tell us if the paintings were old, or lately made. The place, so silent, remote, and smelling sweetly, gave the impression that it had been a sacred spot for long ages, and that not one man but the artists of many generations had come there alone to spend sunny hours, lying on their backs below the rock and daubing it with their coloured clays.

The reconnaissance had revealed nothing and we continued our journey. The river gradually narrowed and the everlasting mangroves gave way to thicker, more varied jungle. Wide plains, covered with long, golden grass, spread away from each bank, and ahead rose a high, rocky wall, which turned opal colour in thc late afternoon light. This rock, we felt, must end our journey - something different must lie beyond it - but before we could reach it, night fell. The banks became dark walls against a tawny sky, and the river flowed in oily streaks of black and orange. We hastily ran into the first landing-place, and by the time mosquito nets and burlap stretchers were up, a fire made, and the billy boiling, the stars were out. With the stars came the mosquitoes - big grey "up-enders," that stood on their heads to bite and looked like bits of grey feather. They were very deliberate in their biting, far more easily caught than the sophisticated little black mosquitoes of Darwin.

The great problem of camping-out in the Northern Territory during the dry season is how to keep warm at night. Our camp on the Alligator was a very cold one. At one o'clock everyone seemed to wake simultaneously, and there was a general stir of chilly persons rolling themselves in blankets and grunting with cold. Then silence again until dawn came. A rosy mist rolled off the plain; there was a movement all through the camp; some onc shouted "Daylight!" and in a moment all was bustle. Wood for a fire had to be collected, breakfast made, mosquito nets shaken free of dew, swags rolled up, and it was eight o'clock before the procession of boats was once more patiently plugging up the river.

This time it was not for long. The wall of rock loomed nearer until at last we were abreast of it, and there on the bank lay a native dug-out and three rough stakes stuck in the mud. This was good enough to be called a jetty. We landed and found to our joy wheel tracks running out to the rocky mountain. While some of the party set out to follow these, the rest of us set fire to the plain. The smoke rushed up into the sky and signalled "white man" to a native camp that was hidden from our eyes. Before long we saw four natives stepping over the plain to meet us-wild, unkempt, unclad creatures, but most welcome to our eyes.

One of them was a youth of about sixteen, whose companions gave his name as Buckley.

His features were almost Jewish in cast, and he had a most engaging expression of wistful candour which now and then gave way to a wondering smile. One of his friends stood apart somewhat morosely, but was distinctly offended when a tactless white asked if he were a myall, or wild black that had not yet come into contact with civilised man. "Me no more myall fella," he said indignantly. As he was smeared from head to foot with wood ash, wore his hair in a high fuzz round his face, and was clad only in a girdle of native string, there was some excuse for the supposition. Buckley's civilisation had only advanced to the extent of saying "yaas " most sweetly to every question put to him; but two of his companions, Governor and Charlie, were quite loquacious and admitted with proud chuckles having been in Darwin gaol. From them we learned to our satisfaction that the canoe and the stakes were indeed Cahill's own jetty, and that the wheel tracks ran straight out to Oenpelli. As to Smith's jetty, it had long ago been washed away, and even in its prime had only consisted of one stake stuck in the mud.

Meanwhile the vanguard of three that had set off to follow the wagon tracks that led across the plain and behind the wall of rock, had arrived after a seven-mile walk at Paddy Cahill's station. The sudden appearance there of three white men, actually on foot, and with no sign of a pack horse, caused much excitement. The blacks rushed up to the house calling "Ballanda, Ballanda" - white man - and the Boss and Missis ran out to welcome the strangers. In a short while Romula was despatched with a note to the rest of us waiting anxiously on the river bank. A few wild blacks had collected round us, and presently one pointed to an object moving towards us in the distance - a black-boy on horseback. As he approached the edge of the creek that wound across the plain, one of the wild blacks suddenly threw up his arms. Romula stopped dead, while the blackfellow plunged into the jungle bordering the stream and vanished. Some little bit of tribal law this must have been that forbade them to meet face to face. This bit of by play, so swiftly passed, seemed strangely full of meaning. It seemed to show that the well-clad rider, the trusted friend of white man, was not in reality living in the same world as ourselves, but in one shared by the naked, ash-smeared savage before him - a world swayed by the thoughts and beliefs of a vanished age.

Romula's note told us that Paddy Cahill and his family were close behind, and by sunset the cavalcade had arrived to welcome the newcomers, and especially the one white woman, the first seen by the women of Oenpelli, Mrs. Cahill and her niece, for three years. By nightfall our fires lit up more white faces than had ever before been seen together on the banks of the river, while outside the circle a whole tribe of natives squatted-men, lubras and piccaninnies and kept up a shrill chatter, discussing endlessly the coming of the strangers to the Alligator River.

The evening meal over, there followed a seven-mile ride back to Oenpelli under the stars, first at a walk across the plain full of deep holes, treacherously covered by long stiff grass; "My word, I've come many a buster here galloping after buffalo," confessed Paddy Cabill; - then at a trot as we passed on to the road that led beneath the wall of rock, looming black and mysterious above us. Every here and there a flare of fire among the trees and a low jabbering of voices attracted us to a blacks' camp. First Paddy Cahill pushed forward, speaking to them in their own tongue, then we followed to gaze upon the vivid little picture. A patch of firelight glowed out of the solid darkness of the bush. It shone on black-bearded men leaning against trees, lit up the smooth shoulders of lubras and the plump limbs of sleepy children huddled together on the ground. The arrival of a new white "Missis" caused great commotion. The blacks thrust handfuls of paper-bark into the flames and held them high to gaze at her, chatter¬ing excited comments. One little lubra, Mechung, was persuaded to show off her accomplishment of teeth-rattling. After a few coy chuckles she began hitting her chin smartly with her two fists, and rattling her teeth till it sounded like the rapid play of castanets. She finished up quite breathless but triumphant.

At last we left the trees and emerged on cleared ground, where we could dimly see the shadowy outlines of the station buildings, dotted round with camp fires. The station yard seemed full of natives. Black hands took the reins, dark eyes stared and white teeth flashed. Stout, grizzled old Marillmac, the capable housemaid, grinned a welcome, and two pretty little girls in scarlet petticoats gazed like a pair of solemn-eyed calves, ready to bolt at the slightest movement on the part of the stranger. Supper beneath a raftered roof and a blazing fire were very welcome, and then followed bed, with the pleasing anticipation of seeing next morning what the place was really like.

Just after dawn Marillmac's head poked round the door with a low hiss of "Missis"; then the voice of Paddy Cahill was heard giving orders that the black-boys were to bring in the horses for our early start back to the river, and in a little while the whole household was stirring. Oenpelli by night had had all the fascination of mystery, but by day it was a hundred times more enchanting. In front of the picturesque bark buildings of the station stretched a glittering lagoon, over which white pelicans swooped and ibises wheeled. High walls of rock, glowing purple in the morning light, overhung it, and on the farther side the sun flashed, on a moving stream of horses galloping swiftly in to the homestead. On the edge of the water rocked a native canoe, and before the house lay the garden where two black-boys were watering the rows of vegetables.

Paddy Cahill has always a fine display in his garden, where flourish cabbages, beans, tomatoes, sweet potatoes, bananas, mangoes, paw-paws and oranges. When he is not working there, he is overseeing the building of native cottages at the back of his own house. These are made of timber and bark, and the design is one of which he is justly proud. The roof projects far, forming a verandah, and there is a wide space left between walls and roof to let in air, and a wide space between walls and floor to let water escape in the wet season. This work keeps the master of the house busy, and its mistress also has no time to be discontented.

"There's the housework and training the lubras and sewing dresses for them," she says, " and then I am so interested in what's going on on the station, I'm always running out to see how things are getting on." And so, though she sees no strange faces for months together, she never feels any desire to live anywhere else, or even to visit more civilised places. The interest of the horses, of the natives, of the station work, the change of season with all the difference it brings in the look of the country and the wild life inhabiting it - these things occupy the minds of the dwellers at Oenpelli, and occupy them worthily. The visitor feels the charm of the place just as strongly, and has a pang of desire for the peaceful, happy life there.

The station yard before our start back to the river was a busy scene. Paddy Cahill had sent out word the night before to the wild blacks to come in early so that we might see them. As we stood watching for their arrival, old Marillmac suddenly dashed past us with a flash of her scarlet petticoat and uttered a long, high-pitched scream of words, ending by flinging her arms over her head with a wild whoop. We followed her gaze to see to whom she was thus signalling, and saw a procession of blacks walking swiftly through the trees. In a short while the yard seemed crowded with them, and the air was full of their high-pitched chattering, the trampling of horses' hoofs, and the shrill shouts of the black-boys. Foremost amongst the wild natives was a grey-bearded warrior known as Harry. He should have been called Henry the Eighth, however, for he had six wives, all of whom he had brought with him. Henry the Eighth was a majestic sight, as he stalked, tall, gaunt, and solemn, across the yard, with his small son and heir perched high on his shoulders, while the six wives, some young and comely, others old and hideous, trailed meekly behind.

Soon the horses were ready and it was time to say good-bye. In that short visit of one night, Oenpelli, its glittering lagoon, its sheltering rocks hiding ancient secrets of black lore amongst their crags, its happy, self-dependent population of white men and women and blacks, had cast an enduring spell. Before long the wall of rock shut it out from view, and Oenpelli had vanished, like some beautiful place visited in a dream, never to be forgotten, and never to be found again.

Photo. Dr. Mervyn Holmes.

THE COUNTRY ROUND OENPELLI HOMESTEAD

8 - PORT ESSINGTON AND ITS RUINS

IT is a strange fact that the Northern Territory, the first explored part of Australia, is to-day the least civilised. Its shores appear to modern eyes just as they did three centuries ago to the old Dutch navigators, and the traveller nowadays, gazing at the spots where Flinders marked on his charts "smoke," "fire," or "thirty-five Indians seen here," may behold the same - a curl of camp-fire smoke rising from thickly wooded shores, or a few dark forms of natives running along a golden beach.

Yet civilisation is trickling in drop by drop, and gradually making its way by slow rivulets through the country. Perhaps someday soon there may be busy harbours along the coasts, and a regular steamer traffic weaving to and fro. When that day comes, the ruins of Port Essington will be recognised as some of the most interesting of Australia's relics, and ships will call there to allow their passengers to see them. As it is, they are hardly ever visited by white men, and very few Australians are even aware of their existence.

It was in 1838 that the Government, having abandoned the Military Settlements of Fort Dundas, in Bathurst Island, and of Raffles Bay, decided to form a new one on Port Essington, a fine harbour in Coburg Peninsula. A detachment of marines was accordingly landed there, bringing with them their stores, ammunition, and cattle, to provide fresh meat. They selected a spot that they considered suitable on a headland of red clay, rising out of the water, named the settlement Victoria, and set to work to make it habitable.

The detachment was under the command of Captain McArthur, whom Huxley, who visited the place in the Rattlesnake in 1848, described in emphatic terms as "a litigious old fool, always at war with his officers and endeavouring to make the place as much a hell morally as it is physically." The commandant cannot, however, be entirely blamed for the failure of the settlement. A failure it certainly was, but this was mainly due to the ignorance of the age, when men had no knowledge of how to adapt themselves to new climates and conditions. The site chosen for the settlement was out of the way of sea-breezes, and beside a lagoon, dry during the cool months, but which must nevertheless have been a breeding ground for innumerable mosquitoes during the greater part of the year. Hence the men suffered much from fever, and many died of it, owing to lack of .proper food and other physical comforts. Yet it is a significant fact that those of the marines who undertook to supply the settlement with game, and spent long days with the natives in the bush, hunting kangaroo, wallaby and wild fowl, remained in perfect health to the end.

Even now, when our means of communication are so developed, the Northern Territory often seems to exist quite apart from the rest of the world. What must it have been in the early forties to those dwellers at Port Essington? These were some of the most stirring times in other countries. Italy was preparing to be reborn a nation, and France was inspiring the rest of Europe with thoughts of a new liberty. Not a ripple from these great movements disturbed the quiet waters of Port Essington, to whose inhabitants the gravest public disaster was a failure in the food supply, the most longed-for event the arrival of a merchant brig or man-o'-war. Not only had they to struggle against isolation, but against the Admiralty's bland ignorance of what that isolation meant. The Paymaster, inditing respectful letters, must often have smiled sourly at their demands. Mr. James of the Admiralty Office, London, wrote more than once to reprimand him for not sending in a report by the 1st of January of every year to inform the office that the regiment at Port Essington was "alive and in solvent circumstances." The reprimand had first to go to Sydney, taking perhaps six months or more to the voyage; then it waited at the Commissioner's Office until some vessel, on its way North, was calling at Port Essington; finally the letter would be opened by the Paymaster, a year after it was first penned in a stately London office by a fussy official, to whom probably Brighton represented remoteness, and who continued to deplore the fact that Port Essington would not report itself to the Admiralty on the 1st of January of every year.

Often when stores arrived, after having passed through the stormy seas of Torres Straits, they would be wet and mouldy and unfit for use. Then in due time, the Admiralty would have to send a dignified enquiry, demanding a satisfactory explanation as to why 947 pounds of biscuits had been condemned, and how the Paymaster had disposed of them. It was not within the Admiralty's powers of imagination to picture the hilarious feast at the blacks' camp that must have followed that condemnation.

It happened more than once that the settlement was left for nearly a year at a time without sign of a ship. A feeling of desperation would seize the inhabitants, a half-formed fear that they had been completely forgotten in the agitation of some extraordinary happenings in the world, were marooned and left to starve without means of escape, Stores would be low, salt meat and flour becoming scarce, boots and clothing wearing out. The worried Paymaster, who had long ago sent a requisition to Sydney for supplies, would be in despair. At last the blacks would run in to the settlement with news that a ship had been sighted. So relief would come, and the Paymaster would receive a letter from the Commissioner's Office to explain that the stores had been duly shipped by the" brig Heroine," but she, unfortunately, had been lost in Torres Straits on her way to Port Essington. During a vessel's stay, the whole settlement would be astir, unloading and tallying stores, landing sheep and cattle, exchanging mails, eagerly demanding news of the visiting crew. With what despondent hearts they waved good-bye to the cheering sailors in the rigging, watched the vessel glide out of sight, and faced the long solitude again. The end came in 1849, when Admiral Sir Harry Keppel arrived in the *Meander* to relieve the garrison. He had orders to demolish the fort and the houses, for fear they should lead to bloodshed between the natives and Malays, who used at that time to trade along the coast; or even possibly induce some other power to form a settle¬ment there. So the small remnant of the detachment, that which had survived fever and ennui, were borne away amidst the wails of the natives, and the ruins of Victoria were left to the bush and jungle, which did their best to wipe out all traces of the failure. Did no one of the company feel one pang of regret as he gazed for the last time on the low red cliff and the strip of sand, where the natives were collected flinging their arms in grief? Or did the regret come later, when far away in the midst of some great city-a sudden spasm of longing for the harsh cry of wild geese over the silent lagoon, and the steady drone of a blacks' corroboree through the velvety tropic night.

There is one living soul in the Northern Territory who remembers the days of the settlement at Port Essington - Jack Davis, a stooping, sightless old blackfellow, the last of his race. Nearly seventy years ago, Jack was an eager, agile, little black-boy, something of a pet with the regiment, who loved to run messages for the officers, to strut alongside a squad of marching men, and imitate their stiff movements at drill. Still he mumbles out the story of the regiment, beginning when "Siggem Bemmer" (Sir Gordon Bremer) first sailed into the harbour, and repeats the names of the officers, dwelling on the wonderful feasts at Christmas. Then his back straightens, a curious change comes into his voice, and he feebly attempts to shout the old words of command-"Shon! Eyes right!" So do the long-forgotten tones of some Cockney Sergeant-Major linger ghost-like for a few years more in the voice of an ancient North Australian aboriginal.

It was a grey day, with a lowering sky, when we steamed up Port Essington harbour, which unfolded to us bend after bend of wooded inlets and sandy bays. We anchored opposite the red cliff, but there was no Union Jack leaping at the head of a fort; no crowd of men ran cheering to the landing-place to greet us. Instead, a canoe shot off from the other side, and came swiftly paddling towards the steamer. By the time our dinghy was lowered, and we had rowed to the shore, the canoe was tied up to a mangrove, and its occupants were standing staring at us from the beach. The master of the canoe was a squat, honey-coloured little man, with beady black eyes. This was Jimmy Kafoa, from the Friendly Isles, once a pearl diver till paralysis threatened him, now a trepanger on these lonely shores. With him were three blackfellows who looked like the Three Ages of Man. There was a skinny boy, with abnormally large hands and feet; a middle-aged man, and a lean grey-beard. They were morose and un-smiling creatures, as if they, too, were affected by the gloom that hung over the place.

Jimmy and his blacks led us up the cliff, and there we suddenly came upon five stone chimneys, standing in a row, desolate among the trees, the ruins of the officers' houses. Five stone chimneys and five wide fireplaces -testimonies to the rigid stupidity of a War Office that stuck to good old ways, and never thought of altering its house designs to suit a tropic climate. They are built of bricks made from a greyish brown stone, and the solidity of the masonry speaks well for the workmanship of these British marines. It is pathetic to think of them, cheery and hopeful, toiling at their work under a burning sun, only to see it half demolished and abandoned after ten years. If indeed, they were amongst those left to see it.

Not far from the officers' houses, a still higher chimney and a wider hearth mark the Commandant's dwelling; and near this, best preserved of all, is the bakehouse. The roof is gone, the four walls are still standing, but smothered in palms and shrubs, and a cotton-bush has pushed its way through the chimney. Of the fort all that remains are the bricks of which it was once made, scattered about amongst the grass and trees.

While we were looking at the ruins the old blackfellow suddenly started off inland, signing to us to follow him. He led us about a quarter of a mile through the bush, in perfect silence, only answering our questions of where he was taking us with a vague motion of his hand. When he came to the edge of a lagoon, glittering through green swamp, he stopped and pointed. Almost overgrown by sprawling bushes and creepers, and overhung by still trees, were five sombre gravestones. They were made of the same dark brick-work as the houses. We could find no trace of names or dates on any; but one, a tall obelisk, seemed to commemorate the death of an officer of importance, and another, a very small square slab nearly hidden in the grass, that of a child. Each grave told of a sad procession of home-sick men, wending its slow way from the settlement to the swampy shores of the lagoon. We stood and gazed at the graves, trying to realise the feelings of those unhappy exiles, cut off so completely from the rest of the world; while the three blackfellows, uncomprehending and indifferent, gazed sullenly at us.

"European woman buried here," said Jimmy Kafoa suddenly. He was quite right. It is known that two of the graves are those of the wife and child of one of the officers. She came with her little daughter to Port Essington, doubtless expecting to find a comfortable, sociable military settlement. A year passed, her baby was born, and both she and the infant died and were buried in this lonely spot. Not far from the cemetery is a pretty little strip of beach, backed by fine tamarind trees. Here the little girl used to play happily in the sand, while her mother sat with folded hands, gazing out on the mournful shores, wondering if she would ever live to pick wild flowers in a cool English forest again.

Just as it looked to her eyes, so the harbour looked to ours. Nothing except that the bush had almost hidden all traces of the settlement, to show that over sixty years had come and gone-sixty years, bringing the rest of Australia civilisation, population, and prosperity. But Port Essington seemed far, very far, from that civilisation; utterly lonely and remote, imbued with sadness, as if lamenting the lives sacrificed in that premature experiment.

REMAINS OF COMMANDANT'S QUARTERS AT PORT ESSINGTON

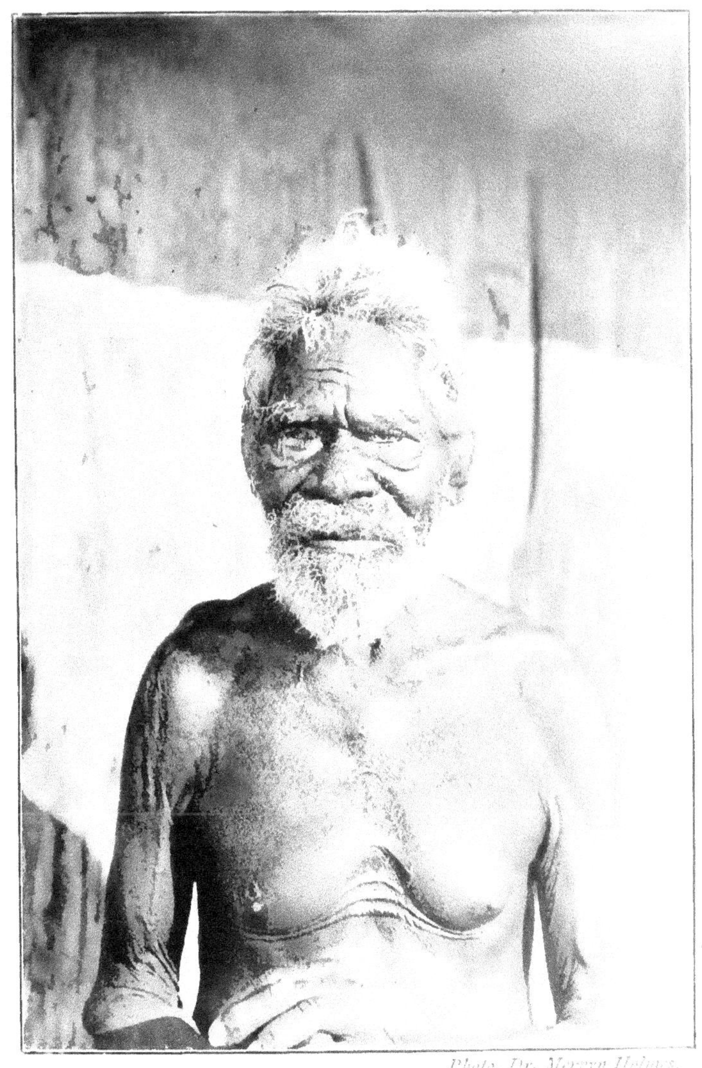

Photo, Dr. Mervyn Holmes.

OLD JACK DAVIS.

THE ROPER RIVER POLICE STATION.

9 - UP THE ROPER RIVER

FROM Port Essington we continued our journey eastwards towards thc Roper River, in the Gulf of Carpentaria, The smooth tropic seas were gone, and we met head winds that set our small steamer plunging. At night we ran into fascinating little anchorages - secret places, closed in by rocky cliffs and golden beaches. Doubtless fleets of brown-sailed Malay proas had made use of them before us; perhaps in the old days some white-winged emigrant vessel had rested a night in their shelter; and now the aged turtles basking on the sand opened their sleepy eyes to the sight of the *Stuart*, snatching a few hours' peace from her turbulent journey.

We pitched all the way towards the Gulf and rolled all the way down it, until we came under the lee of Groote Island-unexplored, mysterious. The moon shone on its low ranges, behind which strange corroborees were being enacted by its black inhabitants, savages still living in an ancient world of their own, into which the vision of a white man had never come. How did they explain to each other the throb of our steamer as she passed by in the moonlight?

The mouth of the Roper appeared in the same way as those of all the rivers along the northern coast-a brimming space between faint lines of mangroves. A native canoe hung about our bows, and we threw down tobacco and tucker to the two naked blacks who paddled it. Our own blacks, known on board as Felix and Tommy, whom we had brought all the way with us from tamer parts, felt for these wild blacks a combination of fear and scorn which it was amusing to behold-fear of their strange magic, scorn of their obvious lack of clothes and other necessities. Felix and Tommy always retreated from the side with a scowl when the canoes appeared, then went below and returned to strut proudly up and down the deck, wearing all the hats and coats they possessed, one on top of the other.

We anchored thirty miles up the Roper, which had become a splendid stream with clear, fresh water flowing over a sandy bottom. It was two o'clock when we anchored, and by six the motor- boats and punts were loaded up and ready to start, The final destiny was Leichardt's Bar, ninety miles up the river, where we were to land most of our party to continue their journey overland. We hoped to reach it next day, spending the night at a Church of England Mission Station thirty miles from where we anchored.

We were a strange procession. First came the motor-boat with most of the passengers. It towed a punt, loaded with the iron parts of a new house for the police at Leichardt's Bar and the baggage of the overland travellers, on the top of which lay stretched their camp cook, smoking his pipe and lolling against bags of flour - the very Prince of Loafers. Behind came another punt, also loaded with stores, in the midst of which stood the overlanders' buggy, its pole reared in air, looking altogether most incongruously situated. At the tail of the procession was a dinghy containing three wild blacks who seized this opportunity of getting up the river. At first progress was very slow. The little motor-boat plugged on bravely, gasping "I've got to go on, I've got to go on," and doing her best to drag the great unwieldy punts. The second of these, the one that held the buggy, behaved very badly, swinging round with alarming suddenness, butting into the one in front, staggering away as far as her rope would let her, and then lurching back again with drunken dignity. At last one of the wild blacks was put in the punt and told to steer. This he did fairly consistently, although, every now and then, unexpected manoeuvres on the part of the buggy-punt told us that he had gone to sleep at his post. "Hey! Wake up that nigger!" the Captain would call; the punt would suddenly come to heel, the motor - boat breathe freely again, and our journey continue more swiftly.

Still we progressed very slowly, and realised that it would be late before we reached the Mission Station. Sunset lit up a low range of rocky hills to a glowing amethyst; the sun sank suddenly, the wild fowl ceased shrieking and clapping. The moon rose and shone on the rippling silver surface of the water, on the great ghostly trees and dark jungle of its banks. Some¬times rifts of white mist trailed across our path, then vanished as we rounded a bend and found ourselves on a wide reach of the river, stretching away to each side like a shining lagoon. It became very cold, and still we went on and on, and saw no sign of a break in the banks to show the clearing of the Mission grounds. Into the midst of the stillness, only intensified by the melancholy call of a night-bird, or the soft splash of an alligator sliding into the water, broke the plunk-plunk of our motor-engine, and the tinkle of a mandolin accompanying a man's voice singing French nursery rhymes. It was the first time that “Malbrouek" and " Ouvre - moi la Porte" had impudently disturbed the great silences of the Roper River.

It was one o'clock in the morning when the Captain declared we were near the Mission. The first mate seized his rifle and fired off a volley into the bank. Clouds of white cockatoos and other fowl burst out of the trees, shrieking in alarm, and for miles around the bush took up the sound, warning the Mission Station that someone was approaching. By the time we reached the clearing, we could discern a line of dark figures standing at the brink of the river ready to receive us. The Captain stood up in the bows. "We are the *Stuart*," he hailed. "All well here?" "No; measles here, " came the answer in a grave stern voice. Our hearts sank, but, measles or no measles, turning back or going on were equally impossible. The risk of infection had to be run, and soon our weird collection of craft was tied up to the bank and we were ashore. There we learnt from the sleepy missionaries that half of the sixty-four children at the Mission were ill with measles, and that they had spent most of the night trying to prevent those who were delirious from rushing to throw themselves into the river.

There was little exchange of news that night, for both missionaries and travellers were anxious for bed. Stretchers were put up as soon as possible, and by two o'clock everyone had turned in. Sleep on a verandah looking out on to an enclosure was short. The missionaries had declared that service would be held at seven-thirty in the enclosure, so rest was broken by the fear of being dis-covered asleep by the congregation, and having to attend the service in bed. At dawn the Mission began to stir. Scuffling, low laughter, and chattering in a mixture of pidgin - English and native speech was heard from the building near, and at last a deep bell clanged out that it was the hour for service. Church was held in the enclosure, round which were grouped the rough Mission dwellings, made of bark, of branches of trees, and of loosely fitting! iron. The congregation was a small one, as nearly all the children were lying wrapped in blankets in an improvised hospital. In the centre stood the head missionary, dressed in white;

opposite him, the rest of the Mission staff and the strangers in rough bush clothes or ship's uniform. To each side were the Mission children, girls in neat cotton dresses, and plump little boys clad only in sarongs made of flour bags, looking demurely down at their hymn-books, and occasionally stealing a sly glance in the direction of the newcomers. In one corner crouched a few myall blacks - those who did not belong to the Mission but who were encamped nearby, and were temporarily working there at herding goats or digging, in return for tucker and tobacco. In the midst of this orthodox Christian service, some of the blacks sat with their hands over their eyes so that they might not see those of their relatives on the opposite benches whom they were forbidden by aboriginal law ever to behold. They all joined in the hymns, singing in sweet tuneful voices. The words they knew by heart, though their meaning was far beyond their comprehension; nor could they even read them, although they kept their eyes fixed on their hymn-books in grave imitation of the missionaries. They listened eagerly to the sermon, and vied with each other in answering questions. Their answers were as often right as wrong, yet it was obvious to the spectators that not real thought, but anxiety to please and aptitude to imitate were what guided them.

The Mission owns two hundred square miles on the banks of the Roper: River, and very largely supports itself, killing its own cattle for meat, growing its own vegetables, and milking its own goats. The work is done by black boys under the direction of the white men, and the girls learn simple housework and cooking. Morning is spent in school, where the children are taught to read, write, and do simple arithmetic. But this part of their education progresses slowly; they read aloud, but do not understand what they read; it is months before they can tell the time, and they seem incapable of composing a letter. If the bush fever seizes the children, as it does at times, they are allowed to go, provided they first ask for permission; should they go without leave, they are punished on their return by being deprived of food. In every case they do come back to the Mission for the tucker and comforts they find there; but, as they grow older, bush -longing will grow stronger, and their lapses into the old savage life more frequent.

The children are a happy, healthy lot, and very easily influenced by the Missionaries. Under their care, they learn cleanliness and other good habits, that will be of use to them as long as white people are there to enforce them. Without that, one feels that in a very short time they would go back to their own ways of living, and to the old aboriginal traditions and customs which arc after all best suited to black nature. The question always arises - are the natives to be preserved for themselves or for us? If the former, the nearer they are kept to the primitive the better; if the latter, then the black stockrider on a station and his lubra who helps in the housework, provided they are well treated, are living far more useful lives than the natives who merely work for their own upkeep on a Mission Station. Yet, whatever differences in opinion there may be, there can be no doubt that much admiration is due to the courage and devotion of those Missionaries who cut themselves off from all friends and comforts to live a life of unselfish endeavour.

A crowd of missionaries and blacks collected on the banks that morning to watch our departure. The boys perched in the branches of the trees, shrieking with delight at the motor-boat and calling excitedly, "Alligater, alligater," as a long grey bulk slid off a spit of mud into the water. A few myalls, spears in hand, squatted in dark groups on the bank, and the crowd was always being increased by little forms wrapped in blankets-refractory patients from the measles hospital who had insisted on coming out to see the fun. We waved goodbye, and the procession set off once more.

The cold moonlight of the previous night was exchanged for dazzling heat, reflected from the surface of the river. The Roper at this part was a broad, clear flow of water, in some parts fifty yards wide. Behind the spiky fringe of pandanus, behind the scaling trunks and feathery trailers of the paperbarks, behind the jungle trees, all mis-shapen and deformed by enshrouding masses of creeper, rose high, firm banks, well grassed and dotted with white-stemmed gum-trees. We passed the junction of two fine tributaries, and finally came to the Bar itself, a chain of rock, over which the river flows at a depth of about a foot. Roper Bar it is called, but Leichardt's Bar is its real name, in honor of the explorer Leichardt, who emerged on it in 1843 on his first fortunate journey through the north of Australia. No doubt as he gazed at the splendid stream of water he said to himself, "In fifty years' time there will be a flourishing town on the banks of this river, the centre of supply to the great pastoral country in the rear. A bridge will span the stream, and small craft will ply up and down, to and from the port at the mouth where large vessels will call from other parts of the continent." If his ghost were ever to visit the spot it would turn away full of disappointment. It would find no bridge, no town, no traffic up and down the river. Instead there is a rough landing, cut out of the banks, and the sole habitation is the police station, a few hundred yards from the edge of the river.

Two troopers live at the station, though nearly always one of them is away patrolling the district, or taking black prisoners in to Darwin to be tried. Their home consists of an iron building with two rooms and an earthen-floored verandah. At the back are one or two out-houses of brushwood, bark, and timber, set round a yard cobbled with stones from the river. One of these buildings is the kitchen, where the policeman bakes the bread and cooks the meal; another is the post office, where the second trooper receives the occasional mail that comes to Roper Bar - ten days' trek from the Overland Telegraph line and three weeks from the railway. Not far from the station is the vegetable garden, an experimental plot where not only pumpkins and melons grow, but where we saw lucerne, wheat, and sorgum flourishing, planted only two months before. There is also an enclosure where the goats herd at night and a horse-yard, for the police station must keep a large supply of horses. Near the river a rough wooden slab carved with the words " C. H. Johnston, speared by Blacks," tells the tale of an early Roper River tragedy.

Two roads lead from Roper Bar, one to the cattle stations of the interior, another along by the banks of the river until it reaches McMinn's Bar, sixty miles farther on, and finally the telegraph line. Not far from the banks of the Roper, on one of its tributaries, stands the homestead of another cattle-run, famous throughout the Territory for the qualities of its mistress. Her husband goes away driving cattle to

Queensland, and she, left with her little son and her blacks, ten days from the Overland Telegraph, not only looks after the house, but manages the station as well. Everyone on the Roper River, from the police to the missionaries, unites in praising her. Her lubras are some of the best trained in the Territory, and the chance traveller is sure of finding there a kindly welcome and a daintily-served meal - not a very easy thing to produce at a moment's notice on an out-back station. We were unlucky enough to find that she was fifty miles from home rounding up cattle, and so we had to leave Roper Bar without having seen the mistress of Paddy's Lagoon Station.

Those of us who were returning to the Stuart could spend only one night at the police station, for we were already more than a week overdue, and our Captain was anxious not to miss the capricious Gulf tide. After dinner, under a roof which we were assured was so eaten by white ant that it might fall upon us at any minute, we sat outside in the moonlight and listened to a gramophone quavering out sentimental songs, to the flying-foxes chuckling in the paw-paw trees, and the murmur of the ripples over Leichardt's Bar.

Night at the Roper River police station meant sleeping in a room whose iron walls were hung all over with varied objects - rifles, revolvers, old felt hats, prisoners' chains, high-boots, and brightly coloured prints of the King and Queen; while on the table was piled an assortment of ancient newspapers, coverless novels, and books of South Australian Police Regulations, all bored through by insects.

Next morning the parts of the new and much-needed house for the police were landed, and the stores for the overland travellers piled on the bank. The rest of us, those who were continuing the journey in the *Stuart,* took our places in the motorboat once more and waved goodbye to our kind hosts, the police, to the overlanders, to the shining rocks and dipping paperbarks of Leichardt Bar. This time, with only empty punts to tow, the motorboat danced gaily down the river, and we reached the Mission Station before night.

At the early service on the following day the Missionary announced the hymn "For those in peril on the sea," adding, somewhat to our dismay, "This is for the Captain and those who are with him." However, a few hours later we reached the *Stuart* without mishap. It was sunset when we turned a bend and saw her lying motionless in the river, looking an Atlantic liner to us in our lowly position in the motorboat. The crew we had left behind crowded to the edge, Tommy and Felix grinned delightedly, and the second mate shouted cheerily, "I've shot six duck for dinner and let the chronometers run down!"

All that night we lay in the river, and, with the first streak of light, made our slow way to the mouth and out once more into the rough waters of the Gulf of Carpentaria.

We steered north-cast for Thursday Island, where we were to coal before returning to Darwin. It was an exciting moment when we sighted a large steamer - the first one we had seen since we started-coming towards us out of Thursday Island harbour. She passed, and suddenly the *Stuart*, which had grown to imagine herself a swift and up-to-date passenger steamer, lost all her complacence and shrank to a small, insignificant coastal craft, slow and out of date.

Thursday Island, on the other hand, had grown. Whereas before, on voyages north, it had appeared to us merely a quaint little port of call, cut oil from the rest of the world, now it seemed a centre of civilisation, a large metropolis swarming with inhabitants.

THE LANDING-PLACE AT THE MISSION STATION, ROPER RIVER.

10 - THE BLACKFELLOW

IN the years to come, when the Northern Territory supports a large white population, there will be much praise given to the pioneers who first opened up the country. There is another helping to-day in their work whose services arc not always recognised the Australian aboriginal. Let us be fair and give him due credit. He, too, is taking his share in the task of blazing a trail for civilisation to follow.

Pioneering is nearly always unconscious.

The white pioneer is not actuated by a wish to benefit future generations, but by the desire to make a fortune whilst living the wild, free life that appeals to him. The black-boy's incentives are tucker and tobacco, but that does not detract from the value of his work. It is the more pathetic that every service he renders the white man today is helping towards the destruction of his own race, and hastening the time when the aborigines of the Northern Territory will be but a myth to the young and a memory to the old.

Must the native of the Territory die out as he has done in the South? So far the same conditions that led to his extinction there 'are to be found here. White man's drink, white man's diseases, neither of which he has the stamina to withstand, have already begun their work of degeneration. It seems as if Nature were determined that the race, which has not toiled by slow ways to civilisation, made mistakes, given sacrifices, shall not be fit to accept its benefits and shall only perish of it. If the blackfellow attempts to leap at one bound the chasm of ages, he will fall and be annihilated. So far the white man has reached out no hand to help him, but only tossed across to him, from his side of the gulf, a stick of tobacco, a box of matches, and a bottle of grog. Now he has suddenly realised his duty towards the race whose land he has taken, and is doing his best to build a bridge for the black man by which he may cross in safety. It remains to be seen if it can be done.

In the most settled parts of the country, where the natives are most in danger of contamination, are established Protectors of Aborigines, under the direction of a Chief Protector, whose office is in Darwin. The Protector of a district sees that all the blacks in the employ of white men are properly treated; he sees that they do not get any intoxicating drink, looks after their health, reports an epidemic amongst them to the Medical Officer in Darwin, and sends any case needing special care to the Darwin Hospital. No one is allowed to employ blacks without a licence, and no one can visit the camp, where they go after the day's work, without permission.

On the outback stations the natives are nearly always well looked after, as, apart from considerations of humanity, it does not pay to ill-treat a black. It is on the points of civilisation, Darwin, Pine Creek, and the mining districts, that the danger is greatest, for it is there that the Chinese are settled. The Chinese are responsible for most of the demoralisation of the natives in the past. They enslave them with cheap grog and opium, to which they fall easy victims. Opium, smuggled into the country by every cunning device, is too precious to the Asiatic himself to be wasted, so, after a few pipefuls, just sufficient to give him the craving, the yellow man only spares the blackfellow the ashes of what he has smoked himself, but it is enough to make him his, body and soul. Hence no coloured man is granted a licence to employ aboriginals and no blackfellow is allowed into Chinatown of Darwin or Pine Creek.

In the future the natives will be kept in certain reserves, and schools will be established where they will learn reading and writing, and the girls will be taught domestic work, and the boys how to carpenter and to labour on the land. What will be the result of this it will be hard to say. At the best it can only be an imitation of civilisation, but, if the aboriginal race can survive for two or three generations, its savage instincts may be replaced by those of a civilised community. The blackfellow must not be led to regard the "Gubment" as a soft-hearted parent, willing to supply innumerable blankets and sticks of tobacco and tucker just for the asking. He must be made to work for what he gets or there is no hope for him.

In the meantime, luckily for those who love the picturesque side of life in the Territory, the aboriginal there is still very far from sophistication. Once away from the railway line and you find him as his ancestors were wild, unclad, scarred all over with cuts full of tribal import, still holding corroborees, still drinking in the wisdom of the white-haired medicine man, still burying his dead in trees, painting crude images on rocks with coloured clays, revering his totem, and imbued with the magic and devilry that he sees in every animal, every water-hole, every manifestation of nature. He does not willingly speak of these things "White man growl, say 'you silly-fella, black-fella,'" so he shyly hides away his beliefs. The few to whom he tells his secrets are not always qualified to pass them on, and were it not for the work of one man, Baldwin Spencer, who has spent months of patient research amongst them, the greater part of their myths, beliefs, and laws would have been lost to science.

The quickness of the average native is a surprise to those who have always heard that the Australian aboriginal belongs to one of the lowest races extant. The blackfellow's mind is that of an absolutely un¬educated intelligent child. He has the same acuteness of observation, the same power of mimicry, the same irresponsible nature, the same unerring sense of justice that tells him whether he is being fairly treated or no. Re is as unhesitating in his likes and dis¬likes, as difficult to compel, as easy to persuade. He respects firmness and invariably takes advantage of leniency; he never cringes, is never servile. He laughs and talks freely with his Boss, and frequently addresses him by his Christian name. One emotion there is of which he knows nothing -gratitude. If some one says to a blackfellow, "Jim, you come longa me to-morra, I give you good fella clothes," he answers casually, "Orright," and accepts them without a word. This is because the blackfellow has never had any idea of saving or putting aside. If he himself is not actually using a possession at the moment, anyone else is welcome to it. A black-boy who is smoking a pipe is given a cigarette; he sticks it behind his ear; a brother native strolls up to him, takes the cigarette, lights and smokes it, not a word passing between them during the transaction. Similarly, if the white man has dozens of suits which he obviously cannot wear all at once, there seems to the black no earthly reason why he should keep them to himself. Things to the aboriginal are things merely, and have no relative value in money or in a future saving of time.

The white man, in self-defence, has had to impose his own laws on the natives, and in consequence there are frequent Court cases of aboriginals charged with cattle stealing, being on a prohibited area, or violence to one of their own kind. At the trial the prisoner is told he must answer "straight fella," and the more civilised he is, the less likely will he be to do so. "Paddy, you bin killem Judy dead fella?" he is asked. "Ya-as, me bin killem dead fella orright," answers the culprit, mildly surprised at such an unnecessary question when he knows that everyone knows he killed Judy. Then follows a term at Fanny Bay gaol, three miles from Darwin. Here he enjoys unheard-of luxuries - good tucker, tobacco, a stretcher, and a mosquito net. During the day he works at the Government Gardens. After release, the prisoner, no longer a myall but well-trained, disciplined, and in the pink of physical condition, may choose to work in town, or he may return as a hero to his own country, where he assumes great airs of superiority and is much respected by those of his tribe who have not yet been "longa Fanny Bay."

The Australian aboriginal has always been a nomad, with no house or patch of cultivation to tether him more to one spot than to another. But the boundaries of his "country," the district within which he wanders, are very sharply defined, and, until the coming of white people he left them at his peril. In each country a totally different language is spoken, and it is quite common to hear two blacks conversing together in pidgin-English. Sooner or later the aboriginal has an intense longing to return to his country, and it is this that makes his labour an uncertain element, for at any moment he may be seized with wandering fever, and announce his intention of going for a "bush walk-about." No power on earth can stop him. The white man, who has just the same desire for change from city life, is forced by circumstances to control it. All the difficulties of luggage and trains and leaving his business make it for him an elaborate matter. But the blackfellow can stalk away at a moment's notice, with nothing but a bundle of spears, and he is provided for. He knows where to find water, where to grub for yams and lily root, how to pull bandicoots out of their holes, how to catch lizards and frogs, how to track and spear kangaroo, how to make fire with two sticks and a stone. He is utterly independent of everything but his own senses, so what is there to keep him back when the bush-longing makes him restless and unhappy?

The supply of black labour can, therefore, not be relied upon, although in times of emergency it has been useful, as, for example, during a strike of white workmen, when a team of aboriginals coaled a Government steamer in wonderfully quick time. Nearly every home has its lubra, who scrubs, sweeps, and washes, and its black-boy, who cuts wood, takes messages, and is generally useful. As you pass by a house, a black shock head and a grin suddenly appear over the fence, and a long thin hand holding a pipe waves you good day. In camp it is always the black-boy who is up before anyone else and away to bring in the horses; it is he who points the way when there is no track. More than once an aboriginal has saved the life of a white man, lost in the bush or dying for want of water. On the outback stations the black-boys, and sometimes the lubras, make splendid stock-riders. One is the black-boy again who patiently waters the station vegetables, carrying the water laboriously in kerosene tins from the river or lagoon. When an extra mail has to be fetched and carried, it is the black-boy who sets off cheerfully on a march of a hundred miles with nothing but a small billy for water, waits only for a meal at the other end, then turns and goes back again, faithfully guarding the precious letters, swimming flooded rivers, and walking quietly into the station yard without a word, after what would have been a heroic journey and a life's adventure to a white man,

No one doubts that the white man is capable of doing these things. It is not that he could not, but frequently that he would not; more often still that he is not there to do them. When in the future the picture is painted of the pioneers - the stalwart, strenuous man and woman pressing on through primeval bush - let there also be depicted marching briskly in their shadow the aboriginal black-boy and his lubra.

Photo, Dr. Mervyn Holmes.

ONCE AWAY FROM THE RAILWAY LINE AND YOU FIND HIM AS HIS ANCESTORS WERE.

11 - BLACKFELLOWS AND MURDER

THE first news of the murder reached us as we were making our way, on board the steamer *Stuart*, towards the entrance of Port Essington. It was a grey day, such as occasionally falls in the tropics. The heavy stillness was stirred only by the beat of our own engines; ahead, across a colourless sea, lay the dull green line of the shore, and to one side the melancholy black fragments of a wreck, stuck on the rocks. Darwin, the nearest point of civilisation, was 150 miles behind us, and we were far from the track of other ships. Suddenly, over the horizon, came fluttering a little grey lugger, which headed straight for the *Stuart*. Our captain, looking through his telescope, made out that she was flying a wisp of red flag half-mast.

Immediately the telegraph on the bridge rattled an order, the throb of the engines ceased, and the *Stuart* waited in silence for the talc of distress coming nearer every moment.

Gradually the figures on the lugger grew more distinct, and as she came alongside wc saw that she was manned by two blackfellows and one white man. We craned over the side of the ship and called anxiously, "What is it? " The two blackfellows gazed up at us stupidly. The white man raised a sunburnt face, fierce with grief and excitement, and shouted hoarsely, "My mate Jim Campbell - speared by blacks at Junction Bay." It was curious what a thrill of rage the words brought to the hearers - a sudden instinctive spasm of hatred of white for black. The lugger swung round the bows of the ship. "Did you bury him?" cried our captain. "His blacks brought him to me; we buried him at King River," shouted the· man in the boat. Then he turned to give a savage order to one of his blacks, who let slip the line; the wind caught the sails of the lugger, and soon she was speeding away with the news over the sea to Darwin.

There was much discussion of the incident amongst those on the Stuart, some of whom had known Jim Campbell himself. "He was one of them cattle-stealers on the Victoria River," said one. "He went to Junction Bay to get out of the way of the police. He used to collect trepang there. Oh, the blacks are not too good at Junction Bay!"

"Who was Jim Campbell? One of the best," exclaimed another with enthusiasm - "one of Australia's best. He got into trouble somewhere inside and came to the Territory some years ago. It's a wonder the blacks didn't get him before. They're not too good at Junction Bay."

'That there was another side to it, the side of these Junction Bay natives, who did not suffer from any excess of virtue, was shown by the remark made by a little South Sea Islander who came aboard at Port Essington. Himself a trepanger, living alone with his blacks hundreds of miles from any dwellings of white men, yet he did not seem at all disturbed by the news. "My friend Campbell, he very rough on blacks," was all he said.

A month later, on the same spot on our return journey, we filed with the police lugger, bound for Junction Bay to find and arrest the murderers. Besides the dead man's mate and blackfellows, there were on board two constables and a Protector of Aboriginals. Her tiny decks looked already crowded, yet she returned later from Junction Bay, 300 miles east of Darwin, with thirty souls on board, nine black prisoners - myalls who could speak no word of English-and fifteen witnesses, among them the wives of the prisoners with their babies. With rough weather, with overladen decks, with the black babies crying all day and all night, the voyage was an unhappy one. At last Darwin was reached. The witnesses were established at the native camp at Kahlin Beach, where they sat all day in a stupor of fear, terrified at the strange blacks chattering strange tongues all around them. The nine prisoners-nine strong young aboriginals of splendid physique - were marched to Fanny Bay gaol to await their trial.

The trial had already begun when we reached the Darwin Court-House. A white man or two, a Chinese dhobie with his bundle of washing, were loitering on the stone verandah, gazing through the wide windows into the court, with its white walls, brown seats, and big red punkah. Facing the door was the dock. On a seat before it sat four of the prisoners, clad in the regulation prison dress of blue shirt and khaki trousers marked with the broad arrow. They held in their hands the end of an ankle chain and gazed sullenly at the floor or out of the door on to the free blue sea. The others were seated in the dock, over the top of which were just visible five close-cropped, egg-shaped heads, five sloping black foreheads, five pairs of gorilla eyebrows. Beside the prisoners stood two' gaolers; near by a Protector of Aborigines: facing them were the Jury. The two counsel, for the Crown and for the prisoners, sat at a table in the centre, while the Judge, in wig and gown, presided over all.

The two constables' first told the story of how they had dug up from the grave at King River the body of the murdered man, wrapped in rugs and a tent fly, dressed in a white shirt and khaki. trousers, with five wounds on his head, arms, and other parts of the body. One curious little incident came to light which showed how the simple ignorance of the black prisoners had led to their own undoing. One night one of the constables had been awakened by two of the men who had heard from other natives that he had been inquiring for them in the district, and had come to see what it was he wanted them for. Poor unsophisticated souls! It was beyond their powers to imagine the series of terrifying events, the bewildering new faces and scenes, and the ultimate sentence to which that action would lead.

The first witness was called Ada - and Ada came slowly walking in and climbed into the witness-box. She was a short, stout lubra, dressed in a blue cotton frock, and a red handkerchief round her neck, curly-haired, with sad eyes, like a dear old retriever dog. Ada not being sufficiently enlightened to kiss the book, the oath was administered to her by the Judge, who said, pointing to the prisoners, "Now, Ada, you savvy those blackfella there?"

"Yaas, me savvy."

"You see those white gentlemen there? " (motioning towards the Jury).

"Yaas, me see 'em."

"All right, Ada. Now, you tell those gentlemen all you savvy about those blackfella. And you talk straight fella."

"Yaas."

"And loud fella."

"Yaas."

Then Ada began to give her evidence as composedly as if she were an expert witness, waiting for the Judge to take down his notes, turning patient eyes on him until he had done so, and explaining points again and again. Gradually, under the examination by Counsel for the Crown, the story pieced itself together.

Ada was not a Junction Bay lubra, but came from Hodgson Downs, farther inland, and she and her "Benjamin," Charlie, had worked for Jim Campbell "four fell a rain."

"That night, all about take kinoo (canoe) go longa Alla" (the native name for Junction Bay). She held up a black hand and began to count on her fingers those that were of the party. "Jim Campbell, Charlie, Dick, Tom Carpenter, old King, old Jinnie, liddle fella Jackie, Nellie, Fred, lubra b'longa him, me, thass all. Bimeby night come. No more moon. Dark fella night. Some fella stop longa camp, some fell a go longa creek, lookout trepang. All about eatehcm light, paper-bark light. Jim Campbell got liddle fella light. He work longa Nellie, liddle fella Jaekie, Dick, Tom Carpenter. Uzzer fella work uzzer side creek. Bimeby Dick go longa kinoo catchem uzzer fella light for Jim CampbelI."

Then came the tale of the sudden attack by myalls. "Blackfella come up, him sing out, 'Ar-r-rh,' like dat. Jim Campbell sing out 'O-oh,' like dat. Him race, then him fall down. All about race longa camp. Bimeby Dick, Tom Carpenter catchem rifle, revolver, go back longa creek, bring Jim Campbell back longa camp. Him dead feIla. Blood here, blood here." Slowly she described the wounds, which of them were made with stone spears, and which with a canoe paddle, touching her own head and arms with light deliberate fingers. The camp mourned over the dead body, and then, "We takem out cloes, shirt, red naga. Bimeby catchem new cloes, white shirt, khaki trousers. Wrappem longa blanket, longa tent-fly, puttem longa lugger."

Here her account ended, for she was not one of those who sailed in the lugger to King River to be present at the burial. Before she left the box, the Counsel for the Defence rose and asked her if she had known old man Nadjimo, who once worked with Campbell.

Photo, Dr. Mervyn Holmes.

THE WIVES OF THE PRISONERS AND THEIR BABIES.

"Yaas, me savvy him before." And the story of Nadjimo then camc out. "Jim Campbell growl longa old man Nadjimo. Bimeby he killem (hit him) longa back, takem dis way (by his leg and arm), puttem longa boiler (boiler for trepang), takem out and kill em longa ground all day. Nadjimo close up dead feIla. He say, 'What for you do dat longa old fella?'"

"And what did Jim Campbell say?"

"Nussing."

With that she left the box, and made way for the next witness, Nellie, a pathetically thin, ugly little lubra, whose mouth was disfigured by a large scar.

"Which way you get that scar, Nellie?" she was asked.

"Jim CampbeIl bin give it me."

"What for?"

"Because I no more look out buffalo hide."

Nellie was one of those who had been searching for trepang close beside Jim Campbell, and she claimed to have recognised two of the attacking blacks, Nundah and Angudyea.

"You bin see 'em longa your eye?"

"Ter-ue, me bin see 'ern longa my eye."

She was told to identify Nundah amongst the prisoners, and turned to do so, whereat Nundah rose proudly with a clanking of chains. He was hastily suppressed by the gaolers, and all nine were made to stand up together. He was not to be daunted, however, and when Nellie was told to identify Angudyea, the irrepressible Nundah leaned forward and eagerly pointed him out. The recognition of the two murderers was therefore rather a failure, and Nellie left the box.

Liddle fella J aekie was a very small and flurried boy of about twelve years. His evidence hardly varied from that of the others. "Blackfella bin come up, sing out, 'Ar-rh.' Jim Campbell sing out 'O-oh,' catchem me longa arm, race longa kinoo. Then him fall down." When he was asked how many myalls there were in the attacking party he turned and began to count the prisoners in the box. But to count up to nine proved too much for liddle fella Jackie, and after much finger work he gave it up and announced to the Judge, "Seven."

Photo, Dr. Mervyn Holmes.

FOUR OF THE MURDERERS.

The best witness of all came next - Tommy Carpenter, a loosely-knit young blackfellow, dressed in a khaki suit with a red handkerchief knotted round his throat. Tommy came striding into the court with a truculent air, mounted the box, and looked round him boldly. All the previous witnesses had spoken in low guttural tones in spite of frequent adjurations from the Judge and counsel to "sing out loud fella." Therefore when Tommy began his evidence in a resounding bellow the whole court jumped.

"You savvy those blackfella?"

Tommy swung round rapidly and roared, "Yaas."

"You see those gentlemen there?" Tommy, too excited to notice that he was asked if he saw the jurymen, not if he was personally acquainted with them, glared straight at them and shouted defiantly,

" No!"

At last the oath was properly administered and his evidence began. He had obviously made up his mind not to be overawed by the court, and when the Judge failed to keep pace with his notes, Tommy showed clearly by his look of contempt how extremely slow he thought him. He told how he and Alec had taken the body in the lugger to King River, where Campbell's mate was working, and buried it there.

"Bimeby we go longa lugger."

"Longa Darwin," put in the Judge.

"Longa Palmerston," corrected Tommy angrily.

Tommy's successor was far milder in manner - Charlie, a Port Essington black, of the parrot-like, strangely Jewish type. He was followed by Dick and by Alec, a stumpy little South Sea Islander, and with them the proceedings of the first day closed. So far there had been no evidence as to the identity of the murderers, and all that the witnesses had done was to describe the scene of the attack. Unconsciously they had made it vividly picturesque - the dark night, the little groups of blacks, with one white man amongst them searching for trepang in the creek by the light of paper-bark torches, so intent that they did not hear the stealthy tread approaching through the mangroves. Then suddenly a rush of savages, wild forms daubed with war-paint, uttering the throaty killing-cry of "Ar-r-rh "; a gasp from the white man as he clutched the arm of the child beside him, the still creek disturbed by the splashing of falling bodies and the hiss of torches hurriedly thrown into the water, then the panic-stricken charge of the blacks back to camp, leaving the dead white man alone in the silence.

There was pathos, too, in the way that the three faithfuls had armed themselves and stolen back to the dreaded spot, returning with the dead body for the camp to mourn over it all that night; in the way that they had washed the wounds, burnt the old clothes, and carefully put on clean ones, then lashed the body into a bundle and sailed away with it in the lugger, to take it to their dead master's mate - the only other white man for so many miles of that lonely coast. Those who behaved so, let it be remembered, were themselves savages, acting on their own initiative, in unforeseen circumstances, with no leader of a superior race to guide them. Not many white people would have acted more promptly, certainly few would have shown such touching fidelity to a master in whose service they had found little reward and much ill-treatment.

When we arrived on the second day a my all lubra was in the witness-box, her baby was howling outside, and Ada was acting as interpreter. Ada stood between the Judge's bench and the box, turning from one to another, uttering first a rapid staccato rush of aboriginal words, listening to the frightened murmurs of the myall, then repeating in low gutturals to the Judge.

On this night the myalls had all been sitting in their own camp.

"Where sun? " asked the counsel.

This was repeated to the myall lubra, who pointed low on the western wal1.

"Close up sun go down," explained Ada. Then, after describing which myalls were in camp, she further related: "Lamareebee say, 'You'n me go killem that one cheeky feIla Jim Campbell. He bin killem my brudder before.' All about put on white paint. Bimeby," continued Ada, interpreting, "all about bin come back.

Bin talk longa me bin killem that one cheeky fella Jim Campbell longa stone spear."

"Who bin talk?"

"Him bin talk himself."

"Lamareebee him talk?"

"Yaas, Larnareebee bin talk," - as much as to say, "You old fool, you know perfectly well who bin talk."

Thus her evidence and that of the lubra who followed definitely incriminated some of the prisoners, for it disclosed their own frank avowal of what had been done.

The old king, who came next, was so decrepit and wandering in his wits that he roused Ada to a great pitch of irritation. He was followed by another myall, who was asked if he knew English. The question had to be interpreted into his own language, and he replied in that language that he did. Last of all came the dead man's mate. He gripped the edge of the box and stared with hard blue eyes straight ahead of him, tense with emotion. It may have been a fierce desire for vengeance, and one can well understand it. Only to hear of the deed had given us an unreasoning thrill of anger. No wonder, then, that to have his dead mate brought to him with five cruel wounds in his body had aroused in him a lasting hatred, just or unjust, against the murderers.

Three of the prisoners, against whom there was no evidence, were discharged with a formal verdict of not guilty. They were freed at once, and left the court looking as if they expected death outside. To all the prisoners the affair must have been utterly incomprehensible and bewildering, and equally so to the witnesses, who were probably quite ready to name the murderers, and could not understand why, instead of all these apparently irrelevant questions, the one simple one was not put, "Who killed Jim Campbell?" and so have done with it.

The Counsel for the Crown now addressed the Jury, bidding them consider the next white men who went out bush in the neighbourhood of Junction Bay. What would happen to them if these blackfellows, convicted on the reliable evidence of their own kind, were let free? And he begged them to do their duty towards God and themselves by returning a verdict of guilty.

The Counsel for the Defence begged them to discount evidence which was obviously only camp-fire jabber, to remember how grossly cruel the dead man had been to the blacks of that country, and to do their duty towards God and themselves by returning a verdict of not guilty.

The Judge summed up, the Jury retired, and after an hour and a half returned with their verdict-five prisoners, Lamareebee, Terandillie, Whardith, Angudyea, Daoolba, guilty of murder; the remaining one, against whom there was no evidence, not guilty.

Some weeks later, a message from the mysterious South commuted the sentence to imprisonment for life, and so Jim Campbell's murderers are now in Fanny Bay, where, as one of their kind expressed it, they have "good fella bed, good fella tucker, good fella cloes, mark longa back allee same emu foot." Even with these luxuries they must often pine for the freedom of their own country and wonder dumbly how it came to pass that they are thus confined.

Who can blame them for what they did?

Who can say they committed a crime in ridding themselves of this cruel intruder into their bush world, who acted towards them with deliberate brutality. Were they not justified in obeying their own moral laws, utterly ignorant as they were that any others existed? It is to be feared that only too often the savage black who commits an act of violence is simply avenging equal outrages done to his own race by the savage white.

A week after the trial the decks of the Government scow Leichardt were crowded with natives - the freed prisoners and the witnesses on their way back to their country with their babies, dogs, and all the possessions they had acquired during their stay in Darwin.

So ends the tale. And yet perhaps it does not end there. It may be that Jim Campbell, no matter what his character, was one of those unconscious pioneers who, in working for themselves, work for their country. His cruelty, the murder of him by these savages with their Stone-Age weapons, the visit of the police and its results - these may be the first flickers of civilisation which will one day shed its full light on the mysteries of that part of the country, now only known as a lonely, inaccessible part, where the blacks are "not too good." If it be so - if by their deed they have let in upon themselves civilisation with its evil effects upon their race - then indeed the death of the white man will be well-too well-avenged.

A strange place it is, this Northern Territory. Like some one whose character puzzles and attracts us and will not be dispelled from our minds, she holds sway by the very problems she invites the white man to solve. They will be solved and she will be tamed and subdued. But, great and prosperous as she will be then, her power to hold will not be stronger then than it is now in her days of almost primitive savagery.

During the coming years the dwellers in the Territory will see great changes. With the extension of the railway and the development of the mines a white population will settle and multiply. The last Asiatics will die or return to their homes and the strange flavour of the East will pass away. No longer in a nook among the ranges will one come upon a little brushwood Chinese hut, with red paper prayers stuck over the door, blue jars glimmering faintly through a smoky interior, and the owner chattering a voluble greeting from the threshold. No longer, from between rows of pineapples, will the lean figure of a Chinese market gardener, with peaked straw hat and glistening copper body, straighten itself to watch the strangers pass; or a crowd of gaudily dressed China boys and girls, like a flock of bright parroquets, run to the gate to call "To shin." The aboriginal, too, restrained and educated, his race dwindling, must lose much of his present interest, and life in the Territory will not be so picturesque when robbed of his lively personality.

Photo, Dr. Mervyn Holmes.

A NATIVE CAMP OF PAPER-BARK HUTS

Photo, Dr. Mervyn Holmes.

THE WITNESSES ON THE WAY BACK TO THEIR COUNTRY

Elsie Masson was born in Melbourne in 1891. A friend of the explorer Baldwin Spencer, she took a job as a governess in Darwin 1913, where she travelled with Spencer who was then Special Commissioner and Chief Protector of Aborigines. She returned to Melbourne and trained as a nurse during World War 1, where she met the ethnographer Bronislaw Malinowski. They married in 1919, and settled in England Italy. They had three daughters. She died in 1935.

Bronislaw Malinowski, Elsie and daughter Józefa, 1920.